best sex writing
2008

best sex writing 2008

Edited by
Rachel Kramer Bussel

CLEIS
PRESS

Cleis Press Inc., P.O. Box 14697, San Francisco, California 94114
Printed in the United States.
Cover design: Scott Idleman
Cover photograph: Alex Treacher
Text design: Frank Wiedemann
Cleis logo art: Juana Alicia
First Edition.
10 9 8 7 6 5 4 3 2 1

"The Study of Sex" by Amy André was originally published at Colorlines.com, March 2006. "Kink. com and Porn Hysteria: The Lie of Unbiased Reporting" by Violet Blue was originally published at Sfgate.com (*San Francisco Chronicle* website), February 2007. "Buying Obedience: My Visit to a Pro Submissive" by Greta Christina was originally published in *Other,* Issue 12, May 2007. "Surface Tensions" by Jen Cross was originally published in *Nobody Passes: Rejecting the Rules of Gender and Conformity* edited by Mattilda, aka Matt Bernstein Sycamore (Seal Press, 2007). "Absolut Nude" by Miriam Datskovsky was originally published in the *Columbia Spectator,* October 2006. "To Have or Have Not: Sex on the Wedding Night" by Jill Eisenstadt was originally published in *Altared: Bridezillas, Bewilderment, Big Love, Breakups, and What Women Really Think About Contemporary Weddings* edited by Colleen Curran (Villard, 2007). "Sex in Iran" by Pari Esfandiari and Richard Buskin was originally published in *Playboy,* May 2007. "How Insensitive" by Paul Festa was originally published at Nerve.com, April 2007. "Menstruation: Porn's Last Taboo" by Trixie Fontaine was originally published in *$pread,* Fall 2005. "The Prince of Porn and the Junk-Food Queen" by Gael Greene was originally published in *Insatiable: Tales from a Life of Delicious Excess* by Gael Greene (Warner Books, 2006). "Battle of the Sexless" by Ashlea Halpern was originally published in *Philadelphia City Paper,* April 2006. "Double Your Panic" by Kevin Keck was originally published at Babble.com, November 2006. "Stalking the Stalkers" by Kelly Kyrik was originally published in *Penthouse Forum,* January 2006. "Sex and the Single Septuagenarian" by Liz Langley was originally published at Salon.com, December 2006. "Dirty Old Women" by Ariel Levy was originally published in *New York,* May 2006. "The Glass Closet" by Michael Musto was originally published in *Out,* May 2007. "The Pink Ghetto (A Four-Part Series)" by Lux Nightmare and Melissa Gira was originally published at Sexerati.com, January 2007. "The Hung List" from *Hung: A Meditation on the Measure of Black Men in America* by Scott Poulson Bryant (Doubleday, 2005). "Tough Love" by Kelly Rouba was originally published in *Playgirl,* May 2007. "Big Mouth Strikes Again: An Oral Report" by Rachel Shukert was originally published in *Heeb,* Issue 9, Fall 2005. "Dangerous Dildos" by Tristan Taormino was originally published in the *Village Voice,* February 2007.

Library of Congress Cataloging-in-Publication Data

Best sex writing 2008 / edited by Rachel Kramer Bussel. -- 1st ed.
    p. cm.
  Includes index.
  ISBN 978-1-57344-302-9 (pbk.)
  1. Sex--United States. I. Bussel, Rachel Kramer. II. Title.

HQ18.U5B45 2008
306.770973--dc22

2007041390

CONTENTS

Introduction:
One Little Word, Infinite Interpretations

Sex. One little word, so much drama. One little word, so many interpretations, definitions, permutations. For some, sex means ecstasy. For others, it means procreation. For some, it means sin outside the confines of marriage. Many believe that only heterosexual penetrative sex qualifies for that hallowed three-letter word; everything else is either foreplay—or forbidden. For a lot of us, myself included, sex is an ever-changing, ever-evolving set of acts, philosophies, and identities. It teaches us, thrills us, empowers us, confuses us, electrifies us. Sex drives our lives and our lives drive our sex, in all sorts of complex ways. *Pleasure and danger,* as the famous Carole Vance anthology called it.

When I thought about the kinds of writing I wanted to include in this anthology, I knew I wanted to read about the kinds of sex that make the world, not to mention one's head, spin. The kinds of writings that throw our notions of what sex is into disarray. The kinds of writings that will long outlast the chronological year printed on the cover of this book because their meanings and messages will continue to be read, debated, questioned, and answered. These pieces, taken as a whole, give a broader view of sex than you've likely ever considered, dealing as they do with biology, gender, crime, politics, the environment, health, religion, race, and much more.

Here you'll find a wide array of writings about the state of modern sexuality, taking you everywhere from the front lines of erotic activism to insightful analyses of everything from sexuality studies to menstruation porn to naked college coeds. From large publications such as *Playboy, Penthouse Forum,* and *Out* to smaller indie outfits like *Spread, Heeb,* and *Other,* as well as online publications and books, each of these pieces contributes to a whole that shows that sex, the act(s) and the topic(s), is much more complex than most of us give it credit for. Whatever definition you currently have for *sex,* prepare for it to be shattered.

Best Sex Writing 2008 includes two pieces that are very near and dear to my heart. As a Jewish woman with a passion for cocksucking (not to mention Monica Lewinsky), I found Rachel Shukert's "Big Mouth Strikes Again: An Oral Report," a fascinating look at the ways Jewish women's mouths have come to be, in the popular imagination, permanently open. While she offers up a few jokes and puns, she bolsters them with a thoughtful essay that goes way beyond the conventional wisdom. Bloggers Melissa Gira and Lux Nightmare break down the meaning of "The Pink Ghetto," a place where I and many of my peers find ourselves, whether we like it or not, simply because we've chosen to write about that vexing three-letter word that's always stirring up so much trouble.

I've also included several personal essays here because I believe they demonstrate some powerful lessons about how sex plays out in our lives. The sexual karma delivered to Kevin Keck in the form of twin baby girls, after a high school career spent lusting after his own town's version of the Doublemint Twins, is deliciously twisted. Gael Greene takes us back to a headier, more hedonistic time when, freed from her marriage, she could seduce the notorious porn star Jamie Gillis, inching into his supposedly seedy world while reveling in his dirtiness, literally. Journalist Scott Poulson-Bryant, in an excerpt from his excellent study *Hung: A Meditation on the Measure of Black Men in America,* a mix of personal experience and impassioned journalism, asks whether the stereotype of the black man as America's most horny, the one who by his very definition signifies sex, is true or even relevant. These pieces you might very well be able to relate to even if you've never been horny for twincest, had an affair, or been a black man, because the authors' words go beyond their individual circumstances to shed light on the current erotic climate.

And then we've got some more unique territory. Out of all the pieces here, Ashlea Halpern's exploration of the lengths today's eunuchs will go to remove their genitals, "Battle of the Sexless," makes me squirm the most, with equal parts fascination and horror, yet I've reread it now numerous times. There's something appealing and at the same time appalling about this state of affairs that Halpern delves into with a sympathetic eye.

Many of the authors here directly address the politics of sex, and demand that the status quo give way to a broader vision of sexual inclusion. Trixie Fontaine's discussion of piss and menstruation porn is one that, like Halpern's, may make you uncomfortable. And that's exactly her point: while some may find her work abhorrent, others are equally turned on by it, and the fact that capitalism doesn't trump human blood is indeed worth investigating. Tristan Taormino looks at the important issue of phthalates in sex toys, while Violet Blue takes mainstream media to task for its biases when it comes to porn reporting. Ariel Levy's "Dirty Old Women" explores relationships between adult women and teenage boys, asking what it means to be molested when you're male: "For many Americans, being a real grown-up requires a penis. And if you've got that, even if you're only fifteen, you must have the maturity and the manliness to know what you want to do with it—even if that involves intercourse with a forty-two-year-old. Who among us would say the same thing about a fifteen-year-old girl?" Her exploration of the motivations of these teenagers and their seductresses (she calls Mary Kay Letourneau and Vili Fualaau "the poster couple for pedophilia or true love, depending on your point of view") makes us reexamine our assumptions about male sexuality. It's no surprise that Levy's piece also surfaced in a volume of *Best Crime Writing;* the intersection of sex and the law has countless permutations, and it's often to the legal system that we look for answers to help us define what "acceptable" sex is. Elsewhere in this collection, in "Stalking the Stalkers," Kelly Kyrik examines real attempts to catch pedophiles in the act of luring children via the Web.

One of the great new frontiers of sex writing is college newspapers, where sex columnists are starting with a base of knowledge I wish I'd had when I arrived at the University of California at Berkeley, helping educate their fellow students and working out the logistics of sex in print. This new generation is bold, brave, brash, and ballsy, and one of the best and brightest is Miriam Datskovsky, who wrote the *Columbia Spectator*'s "Sexplorations" column. Here, she takes us inside the phenomenon of naked parties on campus, calling bullshit on them, in those precise terms.

For all the jokes, hand wringing, and ink spilled about Paris Hilton, even her recent jail time, we are a country whose consumers made *1 Night in Paris* zoom to the top of the porn best-seller charts, resurrecting an interest in celebrity sex tapes that's seeing burgeoning sales once thought to have gone the way of Pam and Tommy. But what happens when you're an Iranian actress caught fucking on film—or possibly fucking on film? Pari Esfandiari and Richard Buskin investigate the case of Zahra Amir Ebrahimi, who's embroiled in a sex scandal about a tape in which she may or may not star, offering insights into the changes in Iranian culture that have made sex both more and less taboo. The situation has seemingly worsened in recent months; in June 2007, Iran's parliament, in a 148-5 vote, approved a measure saying "producers of pornographic works and main elements in their production are considered corruptors of the world and could be sentenced to punishment as corruptors of the world."

As for the word "Best" in the title, I'm the first to admit that this is a fully subjective call. Sex is everywhere, and I encourage you to read more about it on the growing network of sex blogs and mainstream and alternative publications, or take pen to paper (or fingers to computer screen) and write your own sexual manifesto.

I thought I knew a lot about sex when I started working on this book. I've had dozens of lovers, I wrote a sex column for the *Village Voice* for two and a half years, I'm on staff at an adult magazine, and I have listened to countless confessions of sexual peccadilloes and adventures. But when it comes to sex, we can all learn something, as you'll see from even a brief perusal of the table of contents or by skimming any of these chapters—I certainly did.

Sometimes I think *sex* is a code word for every dirty, naughty, perverted thought anyone's ever had. For some it can be encompassed in a kiss, for others a flogging, a performance, or an intense masturbation session. For others, like that famous maxim about pornography, they know it when they're doing it. Sex is broad enough (and powerful enough) that we will continue to write, talk, and debate about it for centuries to come—when we're not busy engaging in our preferred version of it. When I tell people I write about sex, I can see immediately whether their judgment about me has changed in the second it took me to say it. Most of the time, I don't have time to sit and explain how complex a topic we're talking about. Now, I can just hand them this book, which asks just as many questions as it answers, and hopefully does what good sex should do: leave you wanting more.

Rachel Kramer Bussel
New York City
October 2007

Big Mouth Strikes Again: An Oral Report
Rachel Shukert

Once upon a time, the conventional wisdom was clear. The mouth of a Jewish woman served three purposes, and three alone—to berate, to emasculate, and to ask for money. Blowjobs were not part of the equation, not even in matters of life and death. Take this tired old saw:

A Jewish woman accompanies her husband to the doctor. After the doctor has given him a full checkup, he calls the wife into his office.

"Debbie," says the doctor. "Your husband is suffering from a very severe disease, combined with horrible stress. In order for him to live, I suggest you relax him by performing passionate and complete fellatio on him twice a day, mid-morning and mid-afternoon."

Debbie thanks the doctor and leaves. She goes to the car where her husband is waiting.

"Well?" he asks. "What did the doctor say?"

"He says you're going to die," says Debbie.

Jokes like these have long been considered part of the folklore of the Jewish American Princess, but ever since Monica Lewinsky grinned toothily from the cover of *Newsweek,* the plate tectonics of schlong-sucking have been shifting.

"A Jewish girl and oral sex? I don't believe it!" quipped noted comic and midget Jackie Mason following the Lewinsky scandal.

Believe it. Once known for filing their nails while enduring their monthly intercourse, today the oral prowess of the Jewish woman is the stuff of, if not quite legend, then good-natured, if off-color, assumption. Latinas got back, French women don't shave their pits, Jewish women give great head.

The writing is all over the Western Wall: Elizabeth Wurtzel writing about the "accidental blowjob" in *Prozac Nation,* the Hebrew Hammer's mother urging a little Hebrew Hummer for her boychik over the dinner table in *The Hebrew Hammer,* my old friend Jessica Lieberman famously fitting two cocks in her mouth at once during a particularly rowdy Shabbaton.

How the hell did this happen?

How did Goldie Hawn's pampered princess in *Private Benjamin,* whose husband literally has a heart attack when she puts his dick in her mouth, mature into Barbra Streisand's earthy sex therapist in *Meet the Fockers,* who knowingly unleashes the carnal tigress from Blythe Danner's prim WASP housewife with a little girl talk and an earlobe rub? How did the Jewish woman become the first-chair flautist in the skin section?

And, why do discussions about Jewish female sexuality so often take place in the context of cock-sucking? Is there something essentially Jewish about fellatio? After centuries of massacres, are we the product of some lewd natural selection, in which the copious production of saliva and disciplined suppression of the gag reflex proved the only means of survival? Did thousands of years of circumcised men spare us the unfortunate cheese flavor to which the hapless Gentiles were mercilessly exposed?

Sigmund Freud, the one who gave us a name for our oral fixation in the first place, famously quipped: "Sometimes a cigar is just a cigar." No doubt he would be delighted to know that even today, for Jewish women, a blowjob is never just a blowjob.

"You came to the right girl," says Miki, as we shuttle from coffee shop to coffee shop in Manhattan, looking for just the right amount of air-conditioning. She's not on call today—when her phone rings she jovially informs the caller that she's taking a couple of days off so her vagina can rejuvenate. "I give the best head in New York City," she tells me.

A heady claim, perhaps, but given her knowing laugh, husky voice, and disarming frankness about her proclivities and profession, one I have no trouble believing. If anyone has answers, it's Miki. A veteran of both sides of the sexual spectrum, she shows me her driver's license photo, a relic from her days as sheitel-wearing Hasidic Jew with only a passing resemblance to the alluring blonde before me, dressed in a sequined tank top and silver sandals.

"Okay, so this is the whole deal," she says, popping a piece of Starbuck's brioche in her mouth. "This sucks, by the way. Brioche is supposed to be light and flaky. This is *dreck*."

Miki's large eyes, a deep blue-green, widen in thought: "So this is it. Our mothers shove food down our mouths from the time that we're little. We become very oral. It's something else to eat, you know?"

Could it possibly be that simple? Are Jewish women today significantly more oral than the generation before? Is semen now pareve?

Much has been made of the oral fixation inherent in Judaism and the importance of eating in Jewish culture, and with good reason.

Just listen to the strident slurps and clicks of sucking candy against dentures in the sanctuary of any large synagogue in America once the rabbi begins his sermon. Particular food and ritualized meals are structured into the direct observance of nearly every major holiday. Still, the same mouths that encourage a Jewish daughter, home from college, to "*Eat! Eat! You're a skeleton!*" are the same to cluck theatrically through a mouthful of mandelbrot the moment she's a few pounds past marriageable. On the whole, the messages sent to Jewish women today can hardly be summed up by the phrase: "On your marks, get set, suck!"

"It's not fattening," continues Miki, giggling throatily. "It's protein. Believe me, I swallow a lot of protein."

She had a point. Sucking dick is scarcely a resourceful dieting strategy, but it is a propitious moment indeed when a Jewish woman can simultaneously fill her mouth and keep her figure. It occurred to me that the first time I tasted semen it reminded me slightly of my grandmothers' chicken soup—opaque, salty, and slightly chunky. Suddenly, I never wanted to put anything—penile or victual—into my mouth again.

"Can you imagine if it was chocolate flavored?" asks Miki. "You'd never get those fat Jewish girls off the dick!"

"There's certainly an inherent Semitic connection with ingestion," says Dr. Steven Drukman, a professor of performance studies and queer theory at New York University, concurring with Miki's provisional theory at a genteel cocktail party that night. A generously proportioned glass of low-carb rum punch rests against his forearm. Fair enough. But aren't there other cultures characterized as much by constant eating? One rarely hears about Italian girls on their knees in church basements (unless the story ends in an act of disturbingly creative violence). Miki's words reverberate in my mind: "I suck a cock like I suck the marrow from the bone in the cholent." But the bones of a succulent *osso buco* require similar force. Why should the mouth of the Jewess induce such prurient interest?

For a shiksa, Kristina Grish is remarkably versed in the ways of the Jewish woman, from removing unwanted body hair to selecting the proper fish for any occasion. However, while interweaving personal experience and interviews for her clever dating book, *Boy Vey! A Shiksa's Guide to Dating Jewish Men*, one thing kept coming up (pardon the pun) again and again.

"Most people I talked to said Jewish women are better at giving head," declares Kristina sagely, between bites of a mountainous ice cream sundae at the new soda fountain at FAO Schwarz in Manhattan. "And it's partly that Jewish women have more experience."

"Jewish kids have the venue of summer camp," Kristina continues. "A lot of sexual experimentation goes on there. We [non-Jewish girls] didn't have that. Maybe you went to Girl Scout camp for one summer, but that was it. If you went to religious camp, you were some kind of zealot who probably wasn't going to go there anyway."

It's true. A lot of Jewish girls do go to camp, but many, as I did, prefer to spend their summers peacefully at home, watching cable and smoking marijuana with the descendents of Polish stockyard workers (and yes, occasionally pleasuring them orally, bringing new meaning to the phrase "smoking Pole"). Besides, despite the best (albeit bumbling) efforts of school boards across the nation, haven't we learned by now that adolescent hormones are deeply impervious to any known form of threat, therapy, or bribe? A girl who wants a dick in her mouth is going to want it no matter where she is, and her chivalrous male peers will be only too happy to oblige—in or out of a creaky bunk bed.

Kristina has another thought. "I have a Jewish friend, a really fantastic woman, who said to me, 'You know, we physically have much larger mouths. They're much bigger. There's more room to maneuver.'"

Bigger mouths? That was a new one—even for me. Thanks to the editorial cartoons in *Der Sturmer* and other fine publications over the years, I knew that Jews have big noses, cavernous ears, and gigantic, clawlike hands for stealing money, but I never realized that our mouths were large enough to swallow a Gentile baby whole. (I always assumed we at least had to chew.)

After saying good-bye to Kristina, I spend the entire subway ride home vainly trying to fit my fist into my mouth. Frustrated, I remember my childhood friend, Alison O'Toole, who could stretch her mouth over the wide end of a powerful flashlight, the kind so thick it had a handle.

Clearly, we're not the only people with big mouths, be they literal or figurative. And even if we were, an argument built around a genetic trait (that would necessarily repeat itself in every generation of Jewish women) leaves the twenty or so years when according to prevailing wisdom, our mouths were clamped as tightly shut as a nun's knees, unaccounted for. There had to be something else.

"Yes, Jewish girls know how to use their mouths," says Jamye Waxman, a professional sex educator and *Playgirl* columnist, over coffee one morning in Brooklyn. "Jewish girls are talkers. They're opinionated. They're not shy. But what's behind all those outward manifestations is a confidence level. It starts in childhood. We're not raised with an idea that sex is intrinsically shameful, or that it's wrong to enjoy it. And when you're confident, that affects your sexual performance."

A lack of shame is certainly an excellent groundwork for

healthy adult sexuality. The idea that the act of sex is intrinsically dirty is indeed conspicuously absent in Jewish teachings. But openness, and an often unabashed curiosity about all physical functions, characterizes the Jewish family, and it's not always so sexy. Remember your grandmother's unseemly interest in your bowel movements?

"When I first started going down on guys, I went to my aunt for pointers," says Jamye. "I also think that the stereotype of Jewish girls giving head is indicative of something larger, which is that Jewish girls are more open about sex. I think Jewish girls are kinkier."

Maybe Grandma's interest wasn't so innocent.

Jamye gives sex workshops at parties on behalf of Toys in Babeland, a sex toy store in Seattle and New York, where she used to work. I accompanied her to a bachelorette party at the Midtown Marriot Marquis, where she was giving a workshop to a gaggle of girls from Long Island, Jews all. Jamye, a Jewish woman from Long Island, meshes especially well with this demographic, she tells me. They understand each other.

I am overcome with excitement. *This is it!* I think. *This is like a meeting of some secret cabal.* Like the mujahedeen training camps that linger so indelibly in the paranoiac imagination, here in this nondescript hotel suite we gather for indoctrination. Here might the ancient secrets be found. If the Elders of Zion have a synagogue sisterhood, this is it. I couldn't think of a more perfect spot to once and for all uncover the hidden truth behind the Jewish woman's oral fixation.

Gathered on slate-blue love seats, several girls in their midtwenties consume sparkling wine and Cool Ranch Doritos as Jamye shrugs an enormous tote bag from a tattooed shoulder and unpacks dildos, lubricant, condoms, and cucumbers. At least half of the women in attendance sport impressive engagement rings and looks of barely suppressed panic, none more so than the anxious bride-to-be, whose brow furls with tangible consternation. *Why so worried? Odd*, I scribble in my notebook.

Calmly, Jamye introduces herself.

"Jamye? Waxman!" exclaims an excitable redhead perched on the sofa. "You went to high school with my husband! He came back from his reunion going on and on about how Jamye Waxman is a sex therapist!"

After a few minutes spent on older brothers, Hebrew-school teachers, and guys who cut their lawns, the atmosphere is decidedly more relaxed and Jamye turns her attention to the main tool of her demonstration: a seven-inch cyberskin dildo.

"This is Ricky," says Jamye, stroking its testicles fondly.

"Can I say something?" asks a small woman on the couch (and incidentally, because I am powerless to keep from noticing such things, the wearer of the flashiest engagement ring).

"Sure," Jamye replies. "I want this to be very open."

The woman takes a deep breath: "I hate sucking dick. I gag. I hate it."

WHAT?

A chorus, formidable in its volume and insistence, echoes through the room. "Me too." "It's boring." "I'm not good at it and it's kind of gross." The aversion to dick-sucking is nearly unanimous.

"I did it sometimes at camp. That's where we all met," the girl continues, clutching a Reese's Peanut Butter Cup as she gestures to her companions, "but I mostly did it there because if you didn't, guys would break up with you. I seriously got broken up with like three times because I didn't suck dick enough."

"Penophobia, we called it," offers the married redhead, with a manic guffaw.

"PENOPHOBIA!" shout the others, in giddy unison.

I glance at Jamye nervously. Somehow I have found the only Jewish women on earth unwilling to give head.

"Gagging can be very hot," she offers, addressing the first girl. "It's a pretty sexy message to send to your partner that his cock is so big you choke on it. It's dirty."

She offers some other helpful hints: Use your hands. Use your power. A maneuver known as "The Heartbeat of America" goes over particularly well—a pulse that matches exactly that of our great-grandmothers as they stood at the ship's rail for their first glimpse of the Statue of Liberty. Massage the prostate—it increases the intensity of his orgasm and helps prevent prostate cancer! A more convincing argument to a Jewish man for letting you stick your finger up his ass I've never heard.

"I'm really good at hand jobs!" cries the Girl Who Gags. "I have to be, since I don't give head!"

About thirty seconds later, the Girl Who Gags reveals that she owns a vibrating cock ring.

The session ends. I have learned to roll a condom onto a cucumber with my teeth, but I am still without answers.

Outside, teetering dazedly around the concrete microwave of Times Square, it seemed to me that everyone was eating a hot dog, licking a popsicle, or gyrating an enormous dildo around the inside of her mouth like it was nothing.

I had been researching, thinking about, talking about, and watching the act of fellatio for way too long. My mind was starting to show the strain. I may be Jewish, but I'm also human.

On the long subway ride home, I begin to think about my own sexual preferences. I enjoy giving oral sex. I have been told I am fairly adept. I am generally not squeamish about functions of the body, with a couple of exceptions, but this is hardly unusual. As

Miki put it so succinctly, "I don't think most of the girls that are into cocky and pishy are Jewish."

But I also *talk* about sex, oral and otherwise, a great deal, as did all of the Jewish women I spoke with. Not in a sordid way, but in an honest way, a way that genuinely tries to make sense of sexuality, its many meanings, joys, pitfalls. Jewish women have been at the forefront of this kind of active verbal discourse, from Emma Goldman to Gloria Steinem to Erica Jong. Somewhere along the way, the shrillness became seductive, but the sex was there all along.

"The stereotype of the Jewish woman who is too busy filing her nails to have sex always seemed odd to me," Erica Jong tells me a few days later. Whether the Jewish woman is being painted as frigid or animalistic is beside the point, she continues. Regardless of intent, a Jewish woman's mouth is fraught with sexual meaning.

Perhaps, today, it is a mystical thing, a powerful thing, to be pleasured orally by a Jewish girl. The force between our parted lips is, after all, the same that parted the Red Sea as our forebears marched to freedom.

It's been a long voyage of discovery, and while it may be a while before I can once again gaze upon a penis without a dizzying flurry of analysis, I have discovered a valuable truth. When a Jewish woman gives a blowjob, it means something. The thing itself may vary. It can be an assertion—of power, of selflessness, of confidence or ability. It can be an affirmation, a reclaiming of cultural sexuality or a rebellion against a culture that has rendered her sexless. It can be manipulative or pure, exhibitionist or nostalgic, or it can simply be that she can't go five minutes without using her mouth. It can be all these things at once. More notable is what it isn't: it isn't coerced, and it isn't guilty.

Ultimately, the quest to ascribe a single meaning to the blowjob in Jewish culture is futile—its meanings are multiple, contradictory, and as the vast, moistened schism between the 1970s and today demonstrates, forever in flux.

Just ask the former president who, according to Monica Lewinsky biographer Andrew Morton, joked to his Jewish paramour: "What do you get when you cross a Jewish girl with an Apple? A computer who won't go down on you."

Double Your Panic
Kevin Keck

Cary and Mary Forney were not the most attractive girls in high school—if a poll had been taken I doubt either of them would have made the top twenty-five in a class of two hundred—but, as the only identical twins, their rankings jumped considerably from the average "I'd have to have a few beers to consider that" to the highly coveted "I'd give my right pinky for some of that. Swear to God."

When one stated the desire for "some of that," it was understood that one was speaking in the plural: the Forney sisters (and how that name worked so dreadfully against them in the magically alliterative minds of adolescent boys!) were an item only as a pair. I lay awake many nights in my bed, sweating over the collision of happenstance and divine intervention necessary to sandwich me between the Forney sisters.

Thus the Horny Sisters, as they had been known since the first seventh grader learned the word and sent the definition tittering through the class, were elevated to such a desirable state simply because of their rarity. Oh, plenty of guys bagged the Dellinger sisters in high school, but they were three years apart, and it was always separately. (The Dellinger girls inherited their mother's Playmate prettiness but also their father's competitive streak—he was the football coach at our high school.)

It was common knowledge that to sleep with one sister inevitably meant you would sleep with the other; such was their sibling rivalry, and certainly the reason our football team scored more with the coach's daughters than they ever did against opposing teams. However, the Forney daughters were stalked as a pair—in large part because they were rarely separated.

The Forneys were also a formidable softball force, a pitcher-catcher combo that made our school a serious contender for the length of their reign. I was not the only guy to attend games to watch their four identical double-Ds (oh, the perfection of God's symmetry!) fight against their sports bras. Their father was—as far as I know—at every game. His expression perpetually inhabited that ambiguous area between seriously anxious and mildly angry. He couldn't have been more than forty, but he looked closer to sixty. At the time, I chalked it up to his unfiltered Camels and job at the hosiery mill. What was it about those twins that has harbored in my memory for over half my life now? It has something to do with extremes of desire, I think. If you're a straight guy prone to viewing the world in terms of superlatives, then it is one thing to have a three-way with two women, something else altogether if they are sisters (or Swedish, or—heaven help me!—mother and daughter), and yet something else if they are identical twins. What could be better than two similarly hot women with a dash of incestuous taboo? Triplets, of course. It doesn't take a math wizard to figure that out. Only a Greek god might possibly know the carnal majesty of triplets, but the taste of twins on this earth is, however rare, still a possibility under the right circumstances.

That this desire is real is evident all around us: the Doublemint Twins ("Double your pleasure, double your fun..." Does anyone truly believe that's about gum?), the Coors Light Twins, the Barbi Twins...The sexual myth of twinship is perhaps best illustrated by the manner in which the eighteenth birthday of Mary-Kate and Ashley Olsen was met with a countdown that began years before the actual event. (I live in North Carolina where such a countdown ends at the age of sixteen; our state motto is "First in Flight"— you'd never guess we were speaking in Freudian terms.) The days remaining until the Olsens' legality were scratched off by disc jockeys and frat boys with the cheerfulness of Charles Manson coming before his parole board. At the time, I felt a little sorry for them. In retrospect, I should have felt sorry for their father.

Recently, my wife gave birth to identical twin girls. It was not what I intended when I humbled myself as a boy in church and dared pray for something as exotic as identical twins. Whether or not my prayer made a difference is open to speculation. My friend John says it's chance. My father thinks it's genetics. I do not like to think there is a God, because if there is, he or she has a quirky sense of how the universe should be run, though I can't help but think that the God of my Universe would behave exactly in this manner: meddling in the strange matters of lust and leaving the easier problems of famine, disease, and violence to us.

Incidentally, violence and famine seem like easy problems compared to raising hot twins (my wife is a former Teen Miss South Carolina, and barring the infiltration of too many of my genes, the girls will most likely take after their mother). It's problematic enough that suddenly everything that comes along with a new baby—diapers, food, clothing, orthodontia, et cetera—has been doubled. But let's be realistic: I can plan for all that. That's just about money. What I can't plan for is every football player, every band geek, every long-haired-dope-smoking-slacker (ah, my brothers!) who will be circling my little girls like sexual vultures. (Coincidentally, the sexual vulture who eventually preyed upon the Forney sisters was named Elizabeth—she was a softball player at a rival school, and the three of them were busted in a meth distribution ring a few years ago.)

During my own predatory adolescence I was always baffled as to why the fathers of the girls I dated glared at me as though I were a war criminal. At the time I suspected it was because I was rather...well, faggy. Had I lived in a large city, my long bangs, disposition toward pastel colors, and love of Siouxsie and the Banshees would have attracted absolutely no attention at all. Instead I grew up in a place where the Ku Klux Klan still holds the occasional "parade." Intolerance was as much a part of the landscape as mimosa trees and roadside vegetable stands.

Of course, it's not like I had the privilege of meeting every dad in the county. My dating prowess in high school was so frail that I don't have a representative sample of fathers to go on here: my statistics are culled from only two subjects.

The first girl I ever dated, the very perfectly named Barbie, had to escort me to meet her father; I was still a month away from my driver's license, and this simple fact was probably what caused him to dismiss me with a snort and a shake of the head before he returned to waxing his boat. Without a car, what threat was I? He knew not to take me seriously, and his instinct was correct because Barbie soon dismissed me as well to trade up for a college boy.

Shelley's father sized me up quite differently. I know this because when I arrived to pick her up, the first thing he said was: "I don't like you." I smiled sheepishly and said, "Well, I'm pretty likable." He glared at me. He must have sensed the sexual desperation oozing from my pores. He was a squat man with the arms of a longshoreman, muscles built by labor and not vanity. The way the light silhouetted him in the doorway, he appeared to be a mythical creature with the torso of a gorilla and the legs of a ballet dancer.

"Shelley's still getting ready," he said, and turned away from the door without inviting me in.

I stepped in hesitantly and shut the door behind me. I walked into the living room where Shelley's father was watching "Wheel of Fortune" and took a seat on the couch. The contestants solved two puzzles before he muted the television and turned to me.

"Where are y'all going tonight?"

"The movies."

"What movie?"

"I'm not really sure; we thought we'd decide when we got to the theater."

"Are you really going to the movies?"

I squirmed in my seat; I felt my face go red. I have a terrible tendency to look guilty even when I'm telling the truth.

"Yes, sir."

He nodded when I called him sir and turned the volume back up on the television. I really needed to pee, but I wasn't about to ask Shelley's dad to use the bathroom. I noticed a dried date in a glass case next to me, and it struck me as curious. I said, "Do you make preserves or jam or something?"

Shelley's father looked at me the way you might look at someone who's just defecated on your kitchen counter.

"The date—the fruit." I picked up the little case; he snatched it from my hand.

"That's not fruit. It's an ear." I was quite content to watch

"Wheel of Fortune" in silence after that, as Shelley finished getting ready. Once she had emerged from her bedroom and we were safely in my car, I said to her, "What's with the ear?"

"Oh, my dad was in Vietnam. He doesn't talk about it much, but basically he was an assassin."

Needless to say, our relationship was short-lived, most likely because I refused to pick her up from her house after that first trip.

While I lack any dried ears as deterrents to amorous adolescents, I do own a gun, and as I live beyond the town limits I can legally discharge a firearm at a stranger who is on my property without fear of prosecution. I found that law rather barbaric when I was growing up (particularly when some buckshot sailed my way while I was rolling a yard with toilet paper one Halloween), but it seems a comforting thought now. Of course, the other night I couldn't even bring myself to use a BB gun on the raccoon who's been ravishing my trash and redistributing it about the yard. If I'm defenseless against woodland creatures, what defense can I mount against the tenacious hormones of adolescents?

I suppose I could welcome the potential suitors into my home—a Machiavellian tactic of keeping the enemy close. I might play it like every television dad, forcing the boys through awkward conversations where I interrogate them about their plans for the future. And then I'll tell those would-be Romeos what fine gentlemen they are, what decent values their parents instilled in them, because it's not every guy that would be so understanding about going on a date with twin hermaphrodites.

Patrice, my wife, says I'm overreacting. "Just because we're going to have beautiful twin daughters," she tells me, "doesn't mean they're going to be sluts. It's usually the girls with daddy issues who turn out a little slutty." I don't bother pointing out to my wife that she hasn't spoken to her father in eight years, but instead say, "I've published a book that's primarily about me masturbating—badly. Explain to me how our children will avoid having issues?"

"Don't be silly," she says, not meeting my eyes.

I try to listen to her advice and focus instead on the mystery and wonder ahead. When the news of the twins came, Patrice and I moved out to the country, to the house that was abandoned with the death of my grandparents. I like the house: it's a good, safe place to raise children. I sleep and fuck two feet away from where my grandfather died, and sometimes at night I scoot midway down on the bed and look across my wife's belly where two girls share that rare luxury of not entering this world alone: in the dark, the moonlight washing through the windows, her stomach is a smooth hill of promise at the edge of the dark forest waiting outside.

Battle of the Sexless
Ashlea Halpern

He could've filled three Pepsi cans. Maybe three and a half.

That's how much blood Talula estimates he lost the first time he tried to castrate himself.

Life had hit an all-time low. Depression hung around his shoulders like a lead suit. His libido had spiraled out of control, and he was masturbating as much as five times a day.

So in June 1994, at thirty-seven years of age, Talula made a decision. He'd had enough. They *had* to go. He stripped naked and sat in his tub, Betadine solution in one hand, an X-Acto knife in the other. He doused his genitals with the antiseptic until they glowed amber, then slowly, carefully, slit open his scrotum.

No anesthesia. No alcohol. Nothing.

His fingers searched the bloody pulp for the olive-size testes that had caused him so much torment, but he was starting to feel faint.

In that moment, everything made sense: The times he and his best friend would curl one another's hair and put on makeup. The way he used to tuck his penis between his legs and admire his profile. How he would tie string around his testicles until they changed from red to purple to blue. The countless nights he prayed himself to sleep: "Please, God, please let me wake up a girl."

As the drain swirled with blood, he considered folding up his insides, taking a bath and climbing into bed. Instead, he gritted his teeth and sawed straight through his left testicle.

"I just wanted to see what they looked like," he recalls quietly. "But I'd dug too deep. I'd gone overboard."

With that realization, he wrapped the gory mess in a washcloth, bound it with duct tape and drove eighteen miles to the nearest hospital. The medics in the emergency room treated Talula as an unknown—neither male nor female—but patched him up anyway and sent him for a psych evaluation.

After three years obsessing over the remaining testicle, Talula did it again.

This time he had help from a "certain friend" he had always hoped would finish the job. Talula handed the friend a syringe full of Xylocaine and a Burdizzo, a nineteen-inch tool used to castrate bulls. As its mighty jaws clamped around his scarred scrotum, the pain throbbed like poison darts pricking his every nerve.

And then...relief.

The certain friend, honored to have helped, bowed on his way out the front door of Talula's mobile home, located somewhere along the Minnesota-Wisconsin border.

And Talula, well, he was the happiest person alive.

"It was grand," he says, in between long, audible draws on a cigarette. "I felt like Atlas, not having to carry the world."

Every year, some forty thousand men are castrated in this country for oncological reasons. But in a culture where it takes *balls* to be a man, an emasculated male—even one doing it to save his own life—is viewed with pity and shame. Freud believed that castration was man's greatest fear; the cringing reaction most men have to the very word seems illustrative of that. The vast majority of the medical community (and the community at large) still operates within the XX/XY gender binary; it regards voluntarily castrated males, or eunuchs, as little more than quaint cultural anachronisms.

For Talula to cut off his own testicles throws a wrench in society's idea of what it means to be male—or more profoundly, what it means to be human. Yet whenever voluntary castration enters the public dialogue, it's usually in the form of hypersensational headlines on the eleven o'clock news: *Sex-Crazed Pedophiliac Would-Be Rapist Cuts Off Testicles!!!*

The reality is far more complex.

Only one out of seven people who fantasize about castration ever acts on the desire, and those who do have myriad reasons: some dislike the way testosterone affects their mind and body; some feel powerless in the face of their sexual urges or long for the "eunuch calm," a meditation-like state unimpeded by carnal desire; some do it for aesthetic or cosmetic reasons; some are in the process of transitioning from male to female and view it as a cost-effective step on the road to full sex reassignment surgery; and some submissives consider castration the ultimate sacrifice in a sadomasochistic relationship.

"We are *real* people with real reasons," says Talula. "We live next door, we're down the street, at your work. We have mortgages, credit cards, cars, and grandmothers. We're just people that prefer no sex."

And people who, given the choice, would rather *not* take matters into their own hands.

Talula didn't want to self-castrate, but he felt he had no other option. He was afraid if he told physicians or family members, they'd lock him away forever. He could either do it himself, or not do it.

What Talula didn't realize at the time was that he had a third option awaiting, scalpel in hand, in Philadelphia—the castration capital of the United States.

For nearly forty years, thousands of people have traveled here to have their testicles removed by Dr. Felix Spector, a retired osteopath who had offices in North and South Philly, and around the corner from the Pain Center in the Gayborhood.

Unlike most trans-health professionals, Spector didn't follow the guidelines set forth by the Harry Benjamin International Gender Dysphoria Association, the regulatory body dedicated to the treatment of gender identity disorders. He never required that patients—transitioning or otherwise—undergo psychiatric counseling, take hormones, or live outwardly as women.

The way he saw it, the Harry Benjamin guidelines created too many unnecessary hoops. By the time people saved up enough cash to pay him a visit, they *knew* what they wanted. Spector believed his responsibility was to give it to them, "safely, correctly, and with sympathy."

No questions asked, credit cards accepted.

Spector's website claimed he was "a founder of the field" and possessed "arguably more experience than almost any other doctor" in the treatment of transpeople and men with overactive libidos. He even wrote a handbook on it—the twenty-five dollar cost of which could be deducted from the price of surgery.

When I first interviewed the eighty-nine-year-old doctor, he spoke slowly and repeatedly jumbled names and dates. It was a struggle to hear him over the all-Mozart radio program he was blasting in the background.

Spector was born in Philadelphia in 1917 and graduated from the Philadelphia College of Osteopathic Medicine in 1943. After practicing general medicine in Texas, California, and West Virginia, he moved back to Philly in 1954. Three years later, under dubious circumstances, he performed his first castration on a transsexual in Casablanca.

Word spread quickly about the good doctor who would lop off individuals' testicles at their discretion. Patients described Spector as polite and grandfatherly, with a timid smile and a sly sense of humor—the kind of old man who flirts with pretty waitresses and cracks eunuch jokes to guys about to be castrated.

He was known for loading patients into his red Taurus and taking them on a whirlwind tour of Philadelphia, pointing out historic sites like Independence Hall and capping off with a cheesesteak at Pat's or Jim's. After surgery, he would snap their pictures with a Polaroid camera.

"Proof you lived through it," he'd tease and write their name in the white border.

Business boomed with the advent of the Internet; at the height of his practice, Spector was doing ten castrations a month at $1,600 a pop. For an additional $1,200, he'd also remove the scrotum.

"I saw the need for it," Spector says matter-of-factly. "People pushed me for help and it worked out quite well. Never had any kind of problems."

Chris, a fifty-one-year-old medical courier and former patient of Spector's, tells a different story. From the onset of puberty, Chris remembers feeling distinctly uncomfortable with his body. After years of garroting his testicles with rubber bands, he attempted castration with a Burdizzo. The failed effort left him mangled and more determined than ever. By June 2000, Chris had booked an appointment with Spector.

The night before surgery, Chris checked into a Center City bed and breakfast and shaved his entire scrotal region, just as Spector had instructed. In the morning, a chatty, well-fed nurse in her midforties greeted him upon arrival at Spector's Rodman Street home office.

"I walked in and thought, 'Oh my *fucking* God, what have I done?'" he remembers. "It was somebody's grimy front room with an exam table and a couple of stirrups. Papers and junk all over the place. There was nothing sterile about it."

Chris's first impulse was to turn around and go home, but he hadn't traveled this far to return with testicular baggage in tow.

He signed a consent form, paid the balance due, and nodded when Spector asked him, "Do you know what you're doing? Are you ready to go? Let's do it."

The operation was done under local anesthesia, and ended quickly enough. Though Chris felt uneasy about the bandaging job, he walked the three blocks back to his hotel, rested, and ate lunch. By the afternoon, he was being rushed into the E.R. at Jefferson Hospital on a blood-soaked gurney. Spector had improperly sutured a major artery and Chris was hemorrhaging internally.

The botched castration left him hospitalized for a week and required two corrective surgeries to remove blood clots and necrotic tissue.

"I was a real mess," admits Chris, who says he slipped into a "borderline psychotic" depression after the castration. "I would never want to put anybody through it. I tell the story of someone who thinks they were prepared, but wasn't. All I wanted was that aesthetic thing. I had no concept of the side effects."

Spector castrated George Mayo, an androgynous pet groomer from Maryland, who also felt unprepared for the aftershock. But despite years of surprise hot flashes, he says he's never regretted his decision and doesn't believe Spector led him astray.

"Those who go to Spector already know they want it. I did my research," he says, then pauses. "Maybe I could have done more."

Still, Spector was better than the alternative.

When wannabe castrates could not afford Spector, they would often turn to the very place they found him: the Internet, where there exists a subculture of underground cutters willing to perform guerrilla surgeries in motel rooms, at medical fetish clubs, and just over the Mexican border. Scissors, wire cutters, and livestock elastrators are the main tools in a trade that sometimes uses Listerine as antiseptic and Tylenol for pain. Horror stories of desperate men blowing off their own balls with shotguns are endemic in eunuch culture, which partly explains why health professionals question their sanity. And why, in classic chicken-and-egg fashion, castrates resort to such drastic measures in the first place.

As head of the Eunuch Archive (www.eunuch.org), the Internet's largest support site for the castration-curious, Talula and other active participants try to act as a safety valve, educating visitors on the everyday realities of castration and cautioning them against street cutters.

Madison Abercrombie, a thirty-one-year-old transwoman from rural Missouri, discovered the site too late.

Four years ago, Madison was named Michael and was newly married, working at his family's salvage yard and living the American dream. But one thing haunted him: he hated his genitals.

He tried confiding in doctors and church counselors, but they kept using words like "sick" and "perverse." And while he had heard of Spector's work, he couldn't afford the trip to Philadelphia. Random posts in a eunuch chatroom eventually led him to underground cutter Jack Wayne Rogers, a Presbyterian minister and Boy Scout leader from a neighboring town.

Rogers' emails were short and impersonal, but Abercrombie was impressed by how well he knew the Bible. Rogers agreed to meet him at a motel room in Columbus, where, for seven hundred and fifty dollars, he would remove both his penis and testicles.

The surgery took seven hours and twenty minutes. Abercrombie says there were moments of pain so intense, she could feel the life bleeding out of her.

When Rogers realized the life actually *was* bleeding out of her, he told Abercrombie, "You can go to the hospital—just leave me out of it."

And with good reason—Abercrombie later learned that Rogers had been convicted on charges of obscenity and child pornography, and was suspected in the torture and killing of a twenty-year-old man. The substandard operation left Abercrombie so grossly deformed, it took multiple surgeries to undo the damage. Three weeks ago, Abercrombie took the final step in her transition when a California doctor built her a new vagina.

"If I had not been turned away, if I'd just had some medical help setting goals of getting where I needed to be, it never would've happened," Abercrombie says shakily. "It's a cryin' shame."

After interviewing dozens of people in both the trans and eunuch communities, the consensus is clear: in his heyday, Spector was a godsend to people seeking elective castration; in his latter years, he was a danger. Because the medical community doesn't recognize castration as a legitimate treatment option for non-transmen or transwomen unwilling or unable to comply with the

Harry Benjamin guidelines, voluntary castrates must tolerate indiscretions.

But on January 18, 2002, the Pennsylvania State Board of Osteopathic Medicine declared Spector an "immediate danger to the public health and safety" and suspended his license to practice medicine.

It wasn't the first time Spector had received troubling news.

In the 1940s and again in the 1960s, he was found guilty of performing then-illegal abortions. Also in the '60s, a Philadelphia judge sentenced Spector to two years' missionary work in Africa. Then in 1997, *The Philadelphia Inquirer* indexed his numerous problems with the law, which included falsifying pharmacy records, committing billing irregularities, and performing a castration of "grossly inferior quality." Spector was recently named in a malpractice suit in the Philadelphia Court of Common Pleas; he denies culpability.

Patients with postsurgical complications have come back to haunt him on several occasions, as has another familiar name: Dr. Terrence Malloy. Chief of Urology at Pennsylvania Hospital and Spector's personal urologist, Malloy provided the expert testimony that led to Spector's 2002 suspension.

During regular checkups, Malloy says Spector would ply him for surgical techniques and treatment advice.

"He had the brass ones to say one time, 'Can I come and watch you do an orchiectomy?'" recalls Malloy, who denied Spector's requests to observe what he calls a "totally repugnant" surgery. "It's just common sense—a thirty-five-year-old guy does not want his testicles taken off. That's the *height* of an abnormal psyche."

Spector says he's only under attack because he provided a "nontraditional service" in a profession whose values "were engendered during the Victorian era."

Malloy calls Spector a "quack" and a "butcher," and likens his methodology to assisted suicide: "This was not done for any lofty goal—it was done for money. It's the worst type of victimization [that] preys on the most vulnerable people in the American public."

Beyond ethical queries, the State Board suspension cited two lapses in Spector's malpractice coverage and stated that he was untrained, unqualified, and unequipped to be castrating anyone. As an osteopath, Spector was licensed to perform surgery, but he was also obligated to explain its risks and alternatives to the patient. And while he admits to having no formal urological training, Spector says the standards of the American Board of Urology and the American College of Surgeons didn't exist when he first began his practice.

A State Board attorney who asked to remain anonymous offered this hypothetical situation: "Say you were having chest pains and you go to a surgeon. If he says, 'Let's cut you open and do a bypass,' and doesn't check for angina or try medication first, it's not that he did a bypass—it's that he didn't do all the things he's supposed to do to make sure you were a candidate for it."

Spector never had patients professionally screened for psychological disturbances or suggested they explore a short-term course of chemical castration, which is at least reversible. Sometimes he would tell them to think the operation over and call him back later. Sometimes he wouldn't.

Can a physician be expected to follow standard protocol for a taboo surgery when there are no clear precedents, reliable data, peer-reviewed medical literature, textbooks, or medical experts willing to discuss it?

"Look, all I can say is you can't treat a patient if what they want is crazy," says the attorney. "Accepted practice means knowing when to tell your patient that what they want is wrong."

Dr. Sherman Leis, founder of the Philadelphia Center for Transgender Surgery and one of the country's leading plastic surgeons for trans health care, echoes the attorney's sentiment. Leis follows the Harry Benjamin guidelines on a case-by-case basis, but says he'd never do a surgery that wasn't medically indicated. In fact, he finds the idea abominable.

"There are a lot of sick, psychotic people out there," says Leis of non-transmen seeking castration. "A legitimate doctor doesn't operate on somebody who is psychotic. That's incompetent medicine."

Chico State University anthropologist Tom Johnson and Dalhousie University anatomist and neurobiologist Dr. Richard Wassersug disagree that all voluntary castrates are necessarily psychotic. They've spent years studying and surveying members of the Eunuch Archive and researching the realities of androgen deprivation. Together, they're pioneering the sort of research that will ultimately be reviewed by peers, printed in medical journals, taught in classrooms, and discussed openly between doctors and patients.

That's their hope, anyway.

"You still have doctors recycling prejudices from the Roman Empire, without looking at the very real eunuchs around them," says Johnson. "It's a human propensity to try to put everything into pigeonholes—this or that, either/or—without any consideration of the gradations between. There are not two sexes; there are probably fifty."

Gary Taylor, Shakespearean scholar and author of *Castration: An Abbreviated History of Western Manhood*, concurs; he says eunuchs provide a blueprint for the first post-human. "We're entering a time when the possibilities of genetic engineering mean the potential for changing what it means to be human," says Taylor. "But not everybody is going to accept the implications of our capacity to alter human beings. That's the great philosophical and political problem of our future."

Until that day comes, people eke through the system whatever way they can.

Social workers at Philadelphia's Mazzoni Center for LGBT Health and Well-Being have taken a harm-reduction approach, providing patients with nonjudgmental counseling and informational resources.

"We should be able to recognize the need and push for better treatments. Eunuch, gay, trans—doesn't matter," says Mazzoni medical director Dr. Robert Winn. "There should be no backroom abortions."

Sue Collins, Mazzoni's trans patient coordinator, started presenting as a woman three months ago and empathizes with the eunuchs' struggle.

"Everybody says this is the act of a freak, a demon," she says. "So all my life I tried to fight this demon inside me. Then I realized the real demon was society trying to tell me who I am."

When Collins came out as a woman, all but one of her old friends turned their backs. Her ex-wife cut off communication, as have two of their three children. "It's such a tragedy," she says. "Nobody wants this. Nobody wakes up one morning and says, 'Yeah, when I grow up, I want to cut my balls off.' We just want our bodies to fit with our minds and our souls. That's all we want."

Whether it is abortion, alternative cancer treatments, euthanasia, or castration, society must decide where a patient's right to demand an elective procedure ends and where a physician's right to provide ethically acceptable treatment begins. Although many doctors refuse to remove healthy tissue because they view it as a violation of the Hippocratic imperative to do no harm, proponents of elective castration say it's no different than removing extra nose cartilage, unbecoming cellulite, or excess skin on a baby's penis.

Furthermore, they say, physicians have a responsibility to prevent imminent or foreseeable harm. Could it not be argued that rendering a patient's concerns crazy or invalid does the patient greater harm in the end?

"That is the ultimate question," says Paul Root Wolpe, a bioethicist at the University of Pennsylvania and the author of *Sexuality and Gender in Society*. "For some people, the standard of doing no harm requires that the surgeon actually perform the surgery. If they don't, ultimately the patient will undergo greater harm. But that has to be the absolute last step in a long treatment."

Wolpe calls this the "Kevorkian problem": Both Jack Kevorkian and Timothy Quill were advocates of doctor-assisted suicide, but Quill probed his patients in-depth and advocated a strong psychosocial relationship before he'd ever consider lethal measures. Kevorkian helped some patients die within twenty-four hours of meeting them.

"The idea of rampant autonomy ethics, where if you say you want it then what right do I have to ask you questions, is both therapeutically irresponsible and medically spurious," says Wolpe, adding that the moment a patient enlists a physician's help, that physician's moral standing becomes part of the equation. "Any doctor has a right not to perform an act they find unethical. And you don't have a right to compel them simply because *you* find it ethical. When you have a whole profession that finds [elective castration] problematic, you really need to examine why."

Jim, a fifty-seven-year-old eunuch castrated on a friend's kitchen table eight years ago, believes it is a gross double standard. "If a woman went in and said she wanted her ovaries removed, the doctor would say, 'We can set you up on this date and it'll cost you

X amount of dollars,'" says Jim. "Male goes in and says 'I want 'em removed,' it ain't gonna happen. We're left out in no-man's-land."

Speaking as someone who performs sex reassignment surgery but has also been through the process herself, Dr. Marci Bowers of Trinidad, Colorado, says most doctors lack perspective of what it's like to be on both sides of the gender divide: "Their self-esteem is so wrapped up in what goes on with their penis every day, they can't see the forest from the trees."

While Bowers has yet to castrate a non-trans male, she says she would consider it after proper psychiatric counseling. "It's very lonely to hold one of the only flags," she sighs. "But it's God's will. We have the high moral ground in what we're doing."

After the Commonwealth of Pennsylvania officially revoked his license on February 22, 2006 Spector gave up his flag. He took down the website that had given so many disenfranchised men a glimmer of hope, mailed in his wall hangings and wallet certificate, and changed the spelling of his first and last names.

He has taken up residency in a twenty-nine-room Dickensian mansion—rumored to be one of the most haunted properties in Ohio—and spends most of his time cooking, reading medical journals, and renting out rooms to thrill-seeking ghost hunters. He still hears from grateful patients now and again, but says he would just as soon put his past behind him.

During our final conversation (Spector's attorney advised him to cut off contact with *City Paper* after three phone interviews), he tells me he regrets nothing in his controversial career.

"I have no feeling of dread or having done any harm or any wrong," he says in a trembling, world-weary croak. "Philadelphia is full of people ready to tear you apart...[Malloy] has achieved his goal—he put me out of business."

In one sense, he's right. But what's more significant was the hearing examiner's conclusion that castrating patients with no physical or pathological condition added "insult to injury" by exacerbating preexisting psychological problems.

Beyond the courts, Spector's case wasn't helped by Italian filmmakers Gian Claudio Guiducci and Franco Sacchi's 2003 documentary *American Eunuchs*, which provided a damning look at his practice. The eunuch community was outraged by the film, and Spector refuses to discuss it.

He's sick of fighting.

Spector was recently diagnosed with pulmonary fibrosis. His words are garbled in violent coughing fits; it's hard for him to get a word in edgewise. The prognosis is grim, and the doctors at the "big hospital" in Pittsburgh have thrown their hands up.

"There's not a lot of justice in this world," he laughs bitterly. "Not a lot of justice."

What is the future of elective castration with Spector out of commission?

City Paper anonymously called a dozen urology practices in the Philadelphia area to see which, if any, were willing to castrate on an elective basis. Some receptionists reacted with shock and confusion, others as if they'd fielded the question before. One nurse expressed concern that we were taking "a step in the wrong direction."

One phone call, however, garnered very different results.

It was a call placed to Dr. Murray Kimmel, a board-certified urologist with offices located at 2301 Pennsylvania Ave.

"I've made over twelve thousand people happy," Kimmel told us. (Formal calls to Kimmel's office went unreturned.) "People come to me from all over the country, all over the world. I must be doing something right, right?"

According to court documentation and Spector's now-defunct

website, Kimmel was named an "associate" shortly after Spector's license was suspended in 2002; since then, Spector has assumed the role of middleman, making referrals, answering questions, and collecting down payments.

Like his predecessor, Kimmel performs the surgeries on an outpatient basis and demands no psychiatric evaluation, therapists' letters, or waiting period—just two thousand dollars in cash or money orders. He does, however, explain the procedure in great detail, stressing its irreversibility and discussing its aftereffects.

During our phone consultation, he grills us about our personal life (Are we married or single? How old are we? Do we masturbate at work? How many times a day?) and tells us a little about his. (He once received a hand-signed thank-you note from President Eisenhower for teaching sailors how to be urology techs.)

He rambles tangentially, but there is one point he doesn't want us to miss: It's not *his* job to decide what's best for us. If we take the final cut, it's of our own volition.

We tell him we're sold and ask how soon he might be able to squeeze us in. As it happens, someone just cancelled his appointment on Monday. How does 10:00 a.m. sound?

Talula is angry. He has just read an article in the March issue of *Details* magazine with the following headline: "Why Would a Healthy, Normal Man Want to Slice Off His Testicles?" It wasn't the melodramatic wording or thinly veiled sarcasm that irked him so much as the opening anecdote: would-be child molester lusts after little boys, seeks castration to end urges.

"This man is an exception rather than a rule," stresses Talula. "I do not know of one man on the Archive that would want to hurt a flea."

It's publicity like this, he says, that hurts the cause. "We need, as a eunuch community, a medical way to say 'Yes! I want to lose my testicles!' without getting sexual reassignment surgery," says Talula.

But until the medical establishment and society at large are willing to recognize another state of being—the gray area between male and female—Talula and people like him can do little more than boot up, log on and share their own horror stories. That, and hand out Kimmel's direct phone number.

"People will do it themselves if there's not an alternative," he says. "I know. I know because I did it."

Kink.com and Porn Hysteria: The Lie of Unbiased Reporting

Violet Blue

It's no secret that I look at lots of porn for a living, but sometimes I like to spend a little time with people who are a little more obsessed with it than I am, just so that I feel like I have a life outside of the daily bump-and-grind. Mostly, though, I just want to see what the leading antiporn, antihomosexual, pro-life organizations (you know, the ones with pundits on CNN and Fox News and "friends" in the Oval Office) say about my job.

Home of the "ex-gay movement," Pure Life Ministries tells us:

> First, as more hardcore pornography is sold, more is produced, creating a demand for more porn "performers"—many if not most of whom are teens or look like teens. Second, as more "adult businesses" open, there are more public venues for anonymous sexual encounters and the resulting spread of STDs, including AIDS.

Third, as more "adult businesses" open, more neighborhoods in communities large and small are adversely affected. Fourth, as more hardcore pornography becomes available, more youth are exposed to it; and the porn they are exposed to is more violent, degrading and perverse. Fifth, as more persons become addicted to hardcore pornography, more marriages are prevented or adversely affected; and more persons act out porn induced and fueled sexual fantasies—oftentimes in a criminal manner. Sixth, as more persons are exposed to hardcore pornography, more are influenced to adopt its "values" and lifestyles—which contributes to the breakdown of morality.

Al Menconi, from the American Family Association, famous for its activism, informs us: "A number of Christian men have confessed to me that they clicked on a porn site out of casual curiosity. They just wanted to see what the excitement was all about, but they became addicted almost immediately. I'm reminded that serial killer Ted Bundy started on his road to perversion and murder by innocently looking at 'nudie' magazines as a boy. It only took one time for him to become hooked."

And let's not leave out the AFA's Reo M. Christenson, who advises:

> Pornography leaves the impression with its viewer that sex has no relationship to privacy, that it is unrelated to love, commitment or marriage, that bizarre forms of sex are the most gratifying, that sex with animals has a specially desirable flavor and that irresponsible sex has no adverse consequences—no venereal disease, illegitimate

births, abortions, premature marriages, single-parent families or moral erosion. I see no way that a torrent of materials with this subliminal message, which ultimately fans out to reach people of almost all ages, can fail to have pernicious effects. Not that someone sees pornography and then rushes out to commit rape. That may happen, but that's not the main problem.

While what these powerful religious organizations are saying is hysterical (and not in the funny way), I actually don't take much offense at it. They are, after all, religious. We don't expect our religions to be unbiased about sex and porn. However, we do expect it of our media—most especially when it's covering topics close to home.

Last Friday, I received an email from a friend who works at Kink.com, the local porn empire most recently famous for their controversial purchase of the Mission District's historic Armory Building. He was asking me, as a media contact, for advice with a retraction: Canada.com had just published a story citing an erroneous study about the dangers of children's exposure to pornography, using the photo and name of a Kink.com employee at the start of the article.

My friend reminded me that there was a protest at noon against his company's purchase of the Armory Building—and only a few hours later we were exchanging ironic emails about the headline article on SF Gate covering the protest, Steve Rubenstein's "50 Protest Porn Business Inside Old Mission Street Armory." My Kink friend wrote in regard to coping with another round of skewed media hyperbole: "Awesome! They just changed their erroneous caption of the guy washing the outside of the building from doing so in protest since HE WORKS FOR US."

The SF Gate article was little different than this week's *New York Times* piece about Kink and the Armory—yet it is absolutely an outstanding, shining example of the lie of unbiased reporting.

Steve Rubenstein and Jesse McKinley are reporters, and so we require that they report and not serve us with opinion, instead. In both articles, slanted phrases such as "dirty movies" were slipped in like a hostess silently sliding a coaster under your drink—blink and you don't even notice it's part of the judgmental scenery—when a more accurate term like "adult" could serve better. Rubenstein's piece went the distance, making Kink's employees into "manacled performers."

But the most interesting example was the presentation of un-challenged material in the form of quotes from people on the street as antiporn pundits—with no weigh-in from pro-porn pundits. Protesters were quoted as saying, "This neighborhood is already plagued with enough violence and prostitution as it is," and "Kink degrades the neighborhood, degrades women and offers 'dead end' jobs that no decent person would want." Such statements bracket the piece—with no counter-opinions about pornography—and are presented in such a way that readers could interpret opinions as fact. Kink.com was indeed quoted—but only about their use of the space.

This was front-page "news."

Both pieces, from newspapers on opposite coasts of the United States, were wholly typical of journalism's little porn problem. The articles weren't as exciting as the "family" organization quotes about porn, but they certainly attend the same school of thought about the evils of pornography.

Porn is legal in the United States—and no other entertainment industry is as heavily policed and scrutinized by officials. Pornography is made by adults, for adults. It is a job that requires skilled performers who must display enthusiasm for the job. When someone says that porn exploits women, who exactly is being exploited? The lesbian PA? The woman behind the camera? The paid performer? The woman watching it for self-gratification? And who does gay porn exploit?

Saying that porn "leads to harder stuff" is analogous to saying that people who like spicy foods will never be satisfied until they set their tongues on fire (and in the case of the AFA, the tongues of children and farm animals). Saying that porn is only enjoyed by people who "can't have a real relationship" is one of the most hurtful myths. Porn is an excellent way to make yourself feel sexually self-reliant and satisfied between partners, and is frequently enjoyed by couples (together or alone) as part of a healthy sexual routine.

Porn can't "make" anyone do anything: people who molest children and rape will do so regardless of whether a copy of *Edward Penishands* is available for rental or downloading. *Buffy the Vampire Layer* will not make you get an abortion or an STD or become a serial killer. Watch enough porn and you don't want to buy crack or sell five-dollar blowjobs on the corner of Mission and 14th (current activities that are sure to be curtailed when Kink flips on the restored outside lighting). Instead, you'll realize that the true evil of porn is that it's usually just not very good. Porn might give you a few minutes of pleasure, the giggles, outright dismay for poor plastic surgery choices, or sadness that most porn sucks—or it may turn you off completely.

But read enough about how this thinking informs media culture and porn reporting, and you learn something. It was, finally, when I was on the *AFA Journal's* website and reading their advice for giving sermons on the evils of pornography that I had my "turning point." I wanted to see exactly what this organization had to say about biblical advice on how to convince people that porn is bad. One line in the article "Help for Pastors Preaching on Porn and Sexual Issues" showed me the light: "Speaking against porn is rather easy and doesn't require too much tact or intelligence."

So if presenting porn in a negative light, no matter how informally—in print, online or at the pulpit—"doesn't require too much tact or intelligence," then it follows that neither do the people speaking against it.

Praise the Lord and pass the wireless mouse.

The Prince of Porn and the Junk-Food Queen
Gael Greene

I was fascinated by his story. I wanted to know what had led Jamie Gillis, née Jamey Gurman, from a cum laude degree in English at Columbia University and then acting school to reciting Shakespeare while performing live sex at the Show World Center on Eighth Avenue. His father got the name Jamie from Tyrone Power's pirate in *The Black Swan* and that's how he spelled it, but his mother—the two were separated—insisted on Jamey.

"When I check into a hotel, I never know which name to use," he confided. "I feel responsible more and more for Jamie Gillis, since I created him. I had no control over Jamey Gurman. I used to think I was a prince left by mistake. This couldn't possibly be my family." I watched him play Jamie Gillis out in public with me, turning on the self-conscious strut, the velvet confidence of his voice. Inside, I believed he still felt like Jamey Gurman, myopic, unathletic, failing at high school, no one to take to the prom. We were both Cinderella. Immediately, he became that deprived child, Jamey, to me.

Jamey was hungry. His hunger made my hunger seem quite tame. He was fascinated with tasting. He seemed to get an almost sexual thrill—his nose would twitch like a cat's—from a new taste he had never experienced before. His dream, he told me in all seriousness, was one day to invent a fruit.

Does that sound goofy? I thought it was sweet and saw my role in this drama. I would be the cherished facilitator, setting untold delights on his plate, finding my joy in his joy. And he would open an underground world of sexual secrets to me. Granted, he was a porn actor. But here I was, at the peak of my own sexual power. It was just another ascent. So he fucked for money. Not nearly as much money as the women get, but top money for a guy, he boasted. But he had an innocence, a fresh way of looking at things, that I found appealing. And he seemed remarkably happy.

I don't remember ever meeting anyone quite that pleased with himself. He filled his afternoons with pleasure—treating himself to a jar of lingonberries, slipping into a theater with the intermission crowds to see the second act of a Broadway play, signing an autograph for a fan on the street. What a turn-on, especially if the fan happened to be a woman. Evenings, he weighed his options, so many delightful options that he could never be bored. He loved his life. He was in love with his work. He never ceased being amazed that he was paid for making love to dewy young beauties and aging Lolitas. Even his tears were joyful. Telling me about an early love he'd lost when she fell in love with another woman, he began to weep. Then he wiped his eyes and smiled.

"That felt good," he said.

After Don's melancholy and the deep discontent I perceived in Andrew, Jamey's talent for happiness was irresistible. To some people, the adult-film world might have seemed dangerous, a sordid scene with drugs and Mob money. But I saw a rather naïve guy, young for his age but smarter than I would have expected—Columbia, after all, and the *New York Times* with coffee every morning. He'd been moved by a certain passiveness into what seemed easy money, but he appeared no more sexually obsessed than I.

I took him into my world. He looked dashing at the Four Seasons or at Frank Valenza's wonderfully outrageous Palace in that pinstriped brown flannel suit he'd worn in *Misty Beethoven*. I had to be subtle and diplomatic to convince him that the lapels of his shirt looked better inside the jacket, not open and out, à la John Travolta in *Saturday Night Fever*. He liked to wear a shiny floral tie that still had its strip of masking tape inside, labeled *orgy scene*. At gatherings of the lit clique, Gay Talese, immersed then in skinny-dipping research for *Thy Neighbor's Wife,* his monumental opus on swinging in the seventies, was clearly fascinated. Jamey already knew Jerzy Kosinski from grunge cellars of sadomasochism downtown in the Meatpacking District. At the Literary Guild anniversary party at the Four Seasons, they shook hands, grinning, like comrades from a secret sect.

Jamey let me know he had a special girlfriend. She was smart enough to give him freedom to roam, he said. I was seeing him once or twice a week, shamelessly playing to his weakness. I am nothing if not competitive. I dangled Lutèce; he couldn't say no. The Cellar in the Sky at Windows on the World…a different wine with every course. How could he resist? He'd grown up in poverty on West 103rd Street, one of six children. "The only white boy in my PAL group," he said, referring to the Police Athletic League. He dreamed of one day buying the brownstone he'd grown up in and turning it into a castle. "I'd invite everyone I love to live in it," he confided.

"What happened to your acting career?" I asked.

"I am an actor." He was clearly insulted. "I make a living as an actor. Not many actors do, you know. Five percent, according to *Variety*. I really tried to find something I could do, something to care about besides acting. I took an aptitude test. I thought maybe law, or teaching. I almost did get a job once teaching in a school for bad boys." He laughed. "If it had been bad girls, I would definitely have taken it."

"And porn?"

"I was doing Shakespeare Off Broadway for nothing and driving a cab for a living. Then one day, I saw an ad for actors to do nude photos. The job paid forty dollars an hour. That was what I took home for driving a cab all day. And it was easy. It was fun. Everyone was sweet, and I loved the sex."

For a while, it looked as if sex films were getting better and there would be a breakthrough, he said. Everyone in the business talked about serious actors doing explicit sex in big-budget Hollywood films. "I felt good about being in the avant-garde. I felt like a sexual missionary," he told me.

His story was touching. I was impressed by that English honors degree. Originally, he'd gone to Hunter to enroll in classes, but he found the system too confusing, he said. A friend knew an administrator at Columbia. There, registration could be arranged. Second from the bottom in his New Jersey high school graduating class, Jamey found himself uncharacteristically motivated in college.

"At Columbia, I just decided to do it. I was at the top of my class. Got all A's and B's. Everyone said, 'This kid has potential.'" He hesitated, aware that I might think he had squandered his potential. He looked away. "There's a need being unfulfilled in me," he said, turning back with a grin. "That's part of my charm."

That charm was working on me. I felt he'd never really had

a chance. I wanted to do something to help him. I didn't see red lights blinking. Or if I did, I didn't care. I felt I could handle it. I found his dark world intriguing—the movies shot in two days, women rebelling against deeply religious homes and fundamentalist religions, the men mostly Jewish, all of them paid so little in an industry that rakes in millions. He didn't seem to think of himself as exploited. He accepted the limitations; indeed, he was proud that he was among the top-paid men in porn; didn't seem to mind that work was occasional, unpredictable. He was happy. He made just enough money to support an unambitious lifestyle. And oh, the girls. They were so sweet. So "juicy."

"You're like a pig in shit," I said one day. Jamey laughed. "I love what I do." But he was a trained actor, after all, I reasoned. Perhaps all he needed was a little push, a few phone calls to open other doors.

"No one has crossed over from porn to do straight film," he told me. Did he seem dangerously passive? I dismissed the thought. With my confidence and connections, he would get the energy to pursue it, I felt sure.

"I was thinking about writing an article on pornography," I said one evening. "But your story is much more interesting. It should be a book."

"Funny," he said. "Norman Mailer told me the same thing. I met him once at a party. What do you think? Should I let Mailer do my story?"

He wasn't ready to trust me. Too many promises broken, I thought.

Whenever we went to dinner, we'd go dancing after at Regine's or Xenon or the Ice Palace, a dark place with pin lights, butch lesbians, and great disco music. We danced apart, we danced close. Moving slowly to Sinatra, I'd put my hand around his neck, fingers tangled in his dark curls. I find it hard to explain what it was about dancing. The high school wallflower became the queen of the prom. I had great moves. I had the best-looking guy on the dance floor. I was transformed. I had never been good at anything athletic, although I'd always loved to dance, long before disco. Now I was a dancer every night of the week. I could imagine the physical abandon, the elation, the kinetic ecstasy of Cyd Charisse, of Leslie Caron, of Ginger Rogers matching Fred Astaire step by step, only backward (as Gloria Steinem pointed out).

There would be a long line vying to get by the doorman at Regine's. Someone would spot me. "Let Miss Greene in," the hostess would call out. Someone would take my long fur cape and hand it to the cloakroom attendant over the heads of mere mortals patiently queued. I was given no coat check—two hundred coats, but no check for mine.

"It's rude the way the woman who takes your coat doesn't even see me," said Jamey. "She doesn't acknowledge I'm standing there. It's rude to you."

"You're right. I'll say something."

"Don't do it for me. I know who I am," he said. "In my world, no one would know you, either."

Camille, the very blond captain I knew from Le Cirque, would put us at a table up front. Jamey would order Perrier. I would ask for ice water. Camille would bring fancy cookies. And we would wait for the movie star–handsome tuxedo-clad waiters, carnations in their lapels—Regine must have hired a casting director—to push back the screens that hid the dance floor during dinner. Then the DJ would switch vibes from supper-club mellow to jump-around disco. And there was the see-through Plexiglas dance platform, with its pulsating neon.

Jamey never seemed to be in a hurry to get home, unlike other men, normal men with jobs. He so rarely worked, he didn't have to be anywhere at nine o'clock in the morning. As it got later, the after-dinner revelers crowded onto the Lucite floor, anonymous bodies pressing against one another. Jamey closed his eyes, losing himself in the orgiastic intensity of it. I saw his hand brushing a passing chiffoned ass. I let my hand wander, too. He smiled and closed his eyes again. One evening, Elizabeth Taylor danced alongside us, orchid eyes glued to her rangy escort as if he were the next Richard Burton. She seemed to move in a halo of light.

Often, it was two or three o'clock in the morning when we claimed my cape and then walked home. The sex was never hotter than the night Jamey spent dancing inches from the exquisite goddess of his dirtiest reveries, the adolescent Brooke Shields. "Oh, my precious baby," he crooned, eyes closed—but so what?

His world, a crazy world. *I'm writing a book,* I thought. *This is research.* But in fact, I was being naughty and it was fun. I liked doing whatever it took to turn him on. It was hot. I was a new, more aggressive me. I was learning how many women had passed through his life. He spun the tales slowly for my little notebook and the book we'd agreed to write, but, of course, he was rationing his confessions, not sure what I could handle. One day, he spoke of us in the past tense and I got huffy. I realized I wanted to be the one he could never let go. I was sure we had a blockbuster book. "We're going to be very rich," I promised him. The book would bind him to me. I might never be the one woman, but I could be the one woman he really needed.

We were feeding quarters to the porno-flick machines in a cubicle at Show World on Eighth Avenue, a rare afternoon together ("for the book," I'd suggested).

"I remember this film. Oh, these were my babies, my beautiful babies," he moaned, masturbating as he watched himself flanked by what looked like a pair of Lolitas, rubbing against him on-screen. You didn't buy much footage for a quarter. The machine flicked off. He added another quarter. "I can't believe you're taking notes," he said, zipping up to run outside to the cashier for more quarters. Sticky world. I had a new dimension. I did my work. I met my deadlines. I tasted meals not worth writing about and set up photo shoots for the magazine's issue on entertaining. I dated other men. I danced after dinner with other men. But I obsessed about Jamey. My friend Naomi couldn't understand it. "He sounds to me like a giant mouth," she said. Jean-Louis, at Le Cirque, warned me that he could only be trash and might have something contagious. My wise and permissive therapist, Mildred, thought Jamey was just another symptom of my unresolved neurosis. Don was concerned, "though I don't really have a right to be," he said. Why did nobody understand what I saw in Jamey?

Even as an intrepid girl reporter for the *Post,* I had avoided the sleaze of Times Square. And now in the late seventies, the neighborhood was scabrous, full of desperadoes, dealers conducting brazen drug sales on Forty-second Street, scantily dressed runaways from Minnesota in white plastic boots offering themselves on Eighth Avenue. One evening, I found myself trailing Jamey through the tawdry scene, among the child whores and winos, as he stopped at Smile's for the *Times* and his morning grapefruit, my hair soaking wet from nonstop dancing till 3:00 a.m. after some fancy benefit, wearing my mink, my black velvet gown sweeping the pavement.

"Why don't we go to your place?" I said.

"I didn't have a chance to clean," he warned as he led me upstairs to his second-story apartment.

I gasped and stumbled as he pushed the door open, stung by the chaos.

He saw my reaction. "I like it this way. It feels cozy to me."

I took care to avoid sliding on the scattered girlie magazines and underwear. There was a home-movie projector next to the unmade bed, clothes draped and dropped everywhere, a half-eaten baguette, turned to wood now, handcuffs and dildos and lacy panties, a riding crop, a black stocking draped over the bathroom mirror, open jars of strawberry jam and dregs of wine in bottles sitting amid the fan mail on the kitchen table, unwashed plates piled into the sink. A cockroach I pretended not to see skittered away. I wondered how he could dress at night and emerge so pressed and clean from this chaos. It must have some special meaning to him, I thought.

He ignored me, settling into an armchair with the *Times,* an unlit pipe in his mouth. Above him hung a blowup of himself in black leather, a still shot from *Misty Beethoven.*

I stood there in my coat, disgusted, thinking I might leave. I could catch something in the bathroom, I thought. My fur might pick up a cockroach. I was a woman who had amorous adventures in marble bathtubs in five-star hotels. I used lavender soap from Provence and olive oil bars from Les Baux. What was I doing here? I walked to the door. He said nothing. I decided I would stay and not let myself think about it, not let the mess creep me out, not brood about germs or crawly things. I found a hanger for my gown and a couple of wire hangers that would support my coat. In the bathroom, I touched up my makeup and took off the bra and panties I was wearing under a lace black satin teddy. I liked myself in his mirror, breasts billowing immodestly in the deep décolletage, thighs and legs looking very long in high heels and the lace-edged slit of the panties. I walked into the bedroom, kicking aside a high-heeled pump lying on a magazine, and stood there.

Jamey got up from his chair, turned out the lights, lighted the stub of a candle next to the bed with a cigarette lighter. The window shade was up and I could see the marquee of the Martin Beck Theater across the street, visible in the streetlight. Jamey settled the pillows under his head. I caught myself wondering how many times a year he changed his sheets, then shook my head to banish the thought.

I dropped to the bed on all fours and purred. He closed his eyes.

I was in my own porn movie.

Tough Love
Kelly Rouba

After the birth of his second child, my friend Jeff was surprised when his mother-in-law asked him how he has sex in spite of his inability to walk. The quick-witted forty-year-old replied jokingly that he and his wife, Monica, rely on an intricate system of ropes and pulleys in order to pull off the carnal activity.

While the couple hasn't actually resorted to such measures, Monica says she is resourceful in other ways to work around Jeff's limitations.

"There's only one position he can do—being on the bottom," Monica said. "So to have some more variety, we have to have some variations on that. We have to be creative."

Jeff, diagnosed with muscular dystrophy at twelve, said while his condition worsened as he aged, the disease didn't dramatically affect his sexual abilities until a few years ago.

"I could never pick up a girl and do it that way, but I could stand

and do it until I was about thirty-five," Jeff said.

Whether they are in bed or sitting in Jeff's motorized wheelchair, Monica's on top, but "Sometimes Monica faces me, sometimes she doesn't," he said.

Despite his inability to have sex in common positions like missionary or doggy style, Jeff said, "It's still enjoyable because it is Monica. It's more than just sex because we have a connection."

People with disabilities are more likely to achieve sexual fulfillment if they have connections with their partners, or if they are intimate with people who understand the limitations and are willing to work around them.

As a young adult with severe rheumatoid arthritis restricting my mobility, my first sexual encounter with my on-again, off-again boyfriend was satisfactory at best. By our second rendezvous, I wondered if sex would be my downfall in every relationship to come.

Because of my inexperience and my partner's apprehension over hurting me, I never found much pleasure in sex. Our relationship continued sporadically over a number of years, but sex certainly wasn't the highlight.

Although I sought the advice of my physical therapist before losing my virginity, her suggestion to try having sex on our sides proved futile. As I wondered what to do next, my partner took control by pulling me to the edge of the bed and penetrating me as my legs rested on his shoulders. That became our routine position—and even that didn't always go smoothly.

I considered my hips' limited range of motion a major roadblock to having earth-shattering sex, and accepted that intercourse would never be an orgasmic experience for me.

Then I met Adrian.

During our first sexual experience together, Adrian taught me I can handle more than just two positions. We successfully experimented with several, from doggy style to me on top. My confidence grew. The very next time Adrian and I had sex, I had my first intercourse-induced orgasm—and then, a few minutes later, my second.

I took the long, hard road to finding better sex. Since then, I've discovered many resources and programs tailored to the sexual fulfillment of individuals with disabilities.

"There's always ways around the disability," said Dr. Steve Kirshblum, medical director of the Spinal Cord Injury Program at the Kessler Institute for Rehabilitation in West Orange, New Jersey.

Kirshblum's dedication to making individuals with spinal cord injuries aware they can still have fulfilling sexual relationships earned him a spot in the 2005 documentary film *Murderball,* which follows members of the United States Paralympics Wheelchair Rugby Team.

Clips from a video called *Sexuality Reborn,* showing individuals with spinal cord injuries having sex, were also included in the film. "That (video) was one that was done here at Kessler Institute," Kirshblum said. "It's a pretty graphic video for people with disabilities or their significant others."

"Oftentimes in the past, sexuality and intimacy—which are not necessarily the same thing—weren't discussed," Kirshblum said. "There's a lot of information out there. The idea is that one has to look for it."

"Depending on the types of injuries they have, I recommend that people call resource centers that are geared specifically to their type of disability," Kirshblum said. "They'll always have the most up-to-date information for that disability."

Kirshblum also suggests that individuals with disabilities search the Internet, where they can find a bevy of books, videos, and websites sharing ways to achieve intimacy in spite of disabilities. But, he advised, "The person has to discuss this with their healthcare providers to make sure what they are hearing pertains to them."

Writer Tiffiny Carlson offers tips in her bimonthly column under "Tiff's Corner" at www.lovebyrd.com. Carlson, who suffered a spinal cord injury when she was fourteen as a result of a diving accident, also provides advice on a website she hosts called www.beautyability.com.

Carlson says it's important to find a partner sensitive to meeting special needs. Unable to walk, Carlson relies on her boyfriend, Mike Wilkes, to help her transfer into bed.

"It's good to have a partner that's strong, and not everyone is going to find that," Carlson said. "I am not strong, so I need help moving around in bed in different positions."

Carlson also advised finding someone open to experimentation. "I had this partner for four years," she said, "who was really averse to trying new things. Trying new things is what keeps sex fun for me."

Monica and Jeff also recommend trying new locations. Before they had children, the couple said they used to seek out new places to have sex, like the nearby park or her college dormitory's laundry room.

"That was a game we used to play, thinking of weird places," Monica said.

For those resistant to sex outside the bedroom, Carlson said role-playing can spice things up at home.

"It helps you get in the mood," Carlson said, adding that role-playing boosts her confidence since her disability prevents her from being a "dynamo" in bed.

"Foreplay is also essential for people with disabilities," Carlson noted. "Being able to build up [sexual tension] before you have sex helps to increase someone's confidence."

To get in the mood, Adrian and I have done a variety of things, from sending sexy text messages (even when we are two feet away from each other) to playing with vibrators.

While I'm a fan of the Rabbit, Carlson recommends the G-Force silicone dildo. "For me, I have limited mobility in my hands. That's one (dildo) I really like. It's just easy to maneuver."

Carlson said specially designed pillows called Liberator Shapes are also helpful. "They are really good for people who don't move around that good. It allows you to do other positions you didn't think you could."

Eva Sweeney, founder of Queers on Wheels (QOW) and author of *Queers on Wheels: The Essential Guide,* recommends the Flex-O-Pleaser Wand Vibrator because it can mold to any shape.

Sweeney, who has quadriplegic cerebral palsy, started QOW in 2004 to promote the sexual well-being of the physically disabled community through workshops and literature.

QOW welcomes people from all sexual identity groups and aims to empower them with information and support, Sweeney said. Individuals can find information on dating, sex, and ways to adapt sex toys to meet their needs in QOW's resource guide.

Since resource guides and videos don't exactly provide the type of personal attention some individuals are looking for, Carlson said they might want to consider hiring a sexual surrogate.

"A surrogate partner works with an individual who is having difficulty having physical or emotional intimacy," said Vena Blanchard, president of the International Professional Surrogates Association (IPSA).

While Blanchard stresses IPSA is not a sexual maintenance program for people without access to sex, she said a surrogate is trained to help individuals determine what their bodies are capable of sexually, and can help their partners work around limitations.

Licensed or certified team therapists also work with clients, Blanchard said, because "sometimes there is a real need for assistance to help (individuals) overcome internalized resistance to perceiving themselves as sexual because of their disability."

"Sometimes, what we have to do is change our idea about sex," Blanchard said. "When we broaden our concept of sex, then it's more inclusive."

"And if you've got a good partner," Carlson added, "so many things are possible."

Having met Adrian, I can definitely agree.

Dirty Old Women
Ariel Levy

The older woman. Knowledgeable, seasoned, experienced. Hot! The fantasy creature who embodies full-blown female sexuality in all its mysterious glory. Of course, she's out of reach; it will never happen. She inhabits her own complicated realm of emotions and responsibilities and lingerie, and you are just...a kid. But imagine the initiation! The possibilities! (Sexually, sure, but also for bragging.) It would be awesome.

Or would it? What if the impossible happened and she started paying unmistakably romantic attention to you. What if "she told me that she had feeling for me. She told me that she was thinking about me a lot and had feeling for me [and] she didn't know what to do with them," as twenty-four-year-old Debra Lafave told one of her fourteen-year-old pupils, according to his statement to the police. What if you had sex in the classroom? What if she fell in love with you? What if she wanted to marry you? If it stopped being a fantasy and started being your actual sex life, your actual life, would it be thrilling or upsetting? Or both? Would you be scarred for life or psyched for months?

These are questions we've had plenty of opportunities to contemplate lately. A few months ago, thirty-seven-year-old Lisa Lynette Clark pleaded guilty to statutory rape of her son's fifteen-year-old close friend, whom Clark married and whose child she recently gave birth to. In January, a twenty-six-year-old math teacher from Kentucky named Angela Comer was arrested in Mexico with one of her eighth-grade male students (who had allegedly stolen eight hundred dollars from his grandmother for trip money). They had been trying to get married.

Dirty old(er) women do not reside exclusively in states with alligator problems; we have our fair share in the New York area. In August, Sandra Beth Geisel, a former Catholic-school teacher and the wife of a prominent banker in Albany, was sentenced to six months in jail for having sex with a sixteen-year-old, and she has admitted to sleeping with two of her seventeen-year-old pupils. (The presiding judge in the case infuriated the youngest boy's parents when he told Geisel her actions were illegal but that her youngest sexual partner "was certainly not victimized by you in any other sense of the word.") In October, Lina Sinha, an administrator and a former teacher at Manhattan Montessori on East 55th Street, was charged with second- and third-degree sodomy and third-degree rape for allegedly having sex with a former student—who is now a cop—for four years starting when he was thirteen and she was twenty-nine (she denies the charges). And last May, Christina Gallagher, a twenty-five-year-old Spanish teacher from Jersey City, pleaded guilty to second-degree sexual assault of a seventeen-year-old male student.

The story that probably set the most imaginations in motion

is Lafave's. Debra Lafave, a twenty-four-year-old middle-school teacher who looks like a Miss America contestant, is currently serving three years under house arrest for having sex repeatedly with one of her fourteen-year-old male students. After a hearing, Lafave's lawyer, John Fitzgibbons, notoriously said that his client, a former model, was too pretty for jail: "[T]o place an attractive young woman in that kind of hellhole is like putting a piece of raw meat in with the lions." As in several of the other cases, Lafave's beauty and youth blurred the lines of her narrative. What were these stories about? We couldn't tell if they were instances of abuse by adults in positions of power who were badly harming children or if they were *American Pie/Maxim* magazine–style farces about lucky little dudes.

When I was growing up, my father used to say as a joke (sort of), "Teenage boys: the lowest form of life on earth." He was probably imagining some combination of his adolescent self and Philip Roth's Alexander Portnoy, a character who revolved around a tight coil of urge and surge and shame, whose repertoire of obsessions ranged from onanism to defilement and whose actions seemed almost piteously in thrall to his loins rather than his head (which was too busy processing anxiety and guilt to offer much guidance). *Portnoy's Complaint* was a best seller in 1967, but to this day its protagonist is for many people besides my father the epitome of adolescent-male sexuality: desperate, reckless, insatiable. The horny little devil.

If you conceive of teenage boys as walking heaps of lust, you probably conceive of attractive adult teachers who hit on them as public servants in more ways than one.

Media representations of grown women who pursue teenage boys have hardly been scary in recent years. Phoebe's brother on "Friends" married his home-ec teacher and proceeded to live happily ever after. Jennifer Aniston's affair with little love-struck Jake Gyllenhaal in *The Good Girl* would be difficult to describe as abuse. He pined for her, he worshipped her, and if he ended up destroyed, we couldn't blame her…a lost little girl who happened to be in her thirties.

The most famous older woman is, of course, Mrs. Robinson: sinister as well as smoldering, coolly and mercilessly manipulating Benjamin to get what she wants and keep what he wants out of reach. But the fictional figure who is really more representative of our stereotypes is Blanche DuBois in *A Streetcar Named Desire*. Tennessee Williams made her a skittering, simpering hysteric. Where Mrs. Robinson unfurls her silk stocking with utter confidence in her own allure and smoky erotic power, Blanche rushes to cover the lightbulb with a paper lantern so nobody will see the years creeping over her face. (For the record, her advanced age was thirty.) She is desperate for attention and dependent upon the "kindness of strangers," and, it is suggested, she hit on her seventeen-year-old male student because her own maturity was stunted and only a young boy would make an appropriate companion for the young girl still living within her withering skin. By the end of that play, she is raped by Stanley Kowalski, then carted off to the loony bin: a victim.

It's jarring, however, to think of a teenage boy—say, a sixteen-year-old—who's been seduced by a female teacher as a victim. It clashes with our assumptions. A teenage boy who gets to live his fantasy? What can be the harm?

As it happens, that is a very dangerous question. In 1998, Bruce Rind, Philip Tromovitch, and Robert Bauserman (professors at Temple University, the University of Pennsylvania, and the University of Michigan, respectively) published a study that has resounded through the psychological Establishment ever since. The article, published in the American Psychological Association's *Psychological Bulletin,* was what's known as a meta-analysis, an overview of the existing science, in this case on the long-term effects of childhood sexual abuse. The authors concluded that "negative effects were neither pervasive nor typically intense" and that men who'd been abused "reacted much less negatively than women."

Though Rind and his colleagues bent over backward to emphasize the difference between something's being wrong and something's being harmful (it's wrong, for instance, to shoot a gun at someone, even if you miss), the study was spectacularly demonized. Dr. Laura Schlessinger had three psychologists on her show who declared it "junk science." One of them compared its authors to Nazi doctors. The Alaska State Legislature passed a resolution condemning the study's conclusions and methodologies. In May 1999, the Family Research Council along with Tom DeLay held a press conference in Washington demanding the APA retract the Rind study. (Schlessinger was teleconferenced in.)

About a year after the study's publication, Congress passed a formal resolution condemning Rind in an uncontested vote. The president of the APA initially defended the paper and pointed out that it had been peer-reviewed and determined to be scientifically sound, but as the resolution was being debated, he sent a clarification to DeLay saying that child sexual abuse was always harmful and—though the study has never been scientifically discredited—the organization has been trying to distance itself from Rind ever since.

Although it is tempting to assume that the finding that childhood sexual abuse is not as damaging for boys as for girls confirms various widely held beliefs about gender—that boys are tougher and hornier than girls, that males enjoy sex in any form—the issue is more complicated. For one thing, when men seek out sex with underage girls, they are more likely than their female counterparts to have more than one victim and to utilize methods like coercion and threats to secure complicity and secrecy. Women who seek sex with underage boys are more likely to focus on one person and to proffer love and loyalty and a sense of a particular and profound bond. In many of these cases, the woman has floated the idea of marriage.

We (still) like to keep our understanding of masculinity connected to our understanding of maturity. We'd never had a female anchorwoman deliver our news until recently, we don't often let female columnists explain the news, and we've never had a female president to make the news. For many Americans, being a real grown-up requires a penis. And if you've got that, even if you're only fifteen, you must have the maturity and the manliness to know what you want to do with it—even if that involves intercourse with a forty-two-year-old. Who among us would say the same thing about a fifteen-year-old girl?

"For guys, the different issue than for young women is that it's supposed to be the best thing anybody could want in terms of what society is saying or their friends," says Lonnie Barbach, a clinical psychologist and the author of *The Erotic Edge*. "But they don't necessarily feel okay about it, so then they're acting against their feelings. I see a lot of guys with sexual problems who've had that experience. Problems with erections are pretty common, as is anxiety around sex in general." But then, she points out, she only sees the ones who have problems.

It's extremely common for boys who have been molested to be drawn exclusively to much older women from then on. "There is something about early experience with sexuality that tends to stay with you," Barbach says. "A lot of it is by chance. If you are a child who stumbled upon a magazine with women who have very large breasts, you may eroticize women who look like that in adulthood. It's funny, I don't know why it is, but as a child you are just more susceptible." Anything sexual that happens in childhood has a better chance of making a kind of imprint on your erotic consciousness.

Even if we take as a given that it's always wrong for a grown woman to have sex with her teenage students, or her son's friend, or whatever other fifteen-year-old she gets her hands on, a question still remains: why would she want to in the first place?

Teenage boys are not, as a rule, the world's most expert lovers. They are not known for their emotional sophistication or sensitivity. And they do not excel at the tests of masculine status women are supposed to be fixated upon. "If Debra had had an affair with a man who was richer than me, or more successful, that I could have understood," as Debra Lafave's estranged husband, Owen, put it. "But this was a boy. What could he offer her that I couldn't?"

Power, for one thing. Compared with a teenage boy, a woman will almost always make more money. She will always know more about sex. She will generally be more competent and experienced and more able to assert her will on him than vice versa.

If you spend a little time going over stories of grown women who pursue boys, they start to blur together. Often, the woman was a victim of sexual abuse in her own childhood. So in some cases adults' having sex with children is familiar, reiterative. Psychologists say one reason women engage in this is to create a new narrative: If they as adults can have sex with a child in the context of a loving romance (imaginary or real) rather than as an obvious enactment of exploitation, they can then more easily conceive of their own abuse as a love story. To them, the experience of being a gentle perpetrator can be redemptive.

"Sometimes, the woman is not much older psychologically than the boy is in her developmental stage," says clinical psychologist

Judy Kuriansky. "She has arrested development. So she's having sex with a fourteen-year-old, and in her head, she's fourteen, too. She's getting the attention she never got." She's Blanche DuBois. And, Kuriansky says, "there's nothing more erotic that being adored, for women."

Consider the poster couple for pedophilia or true love, depending on your point of view: Mary Kay Letourneau and Vili Fualaau. A review: Letourneau was Fualaau's second-grade teacher, then she taught him again—and had sex with him—when he was a twelve-year-old in her sixth-grade class. She gave birth to their first child shortly before she went to jail. She became pregnant with their second child when she was out on parole. She went back to jail for seven years. After her release, they got back together. Letourneau and Fualaau were married in a televised ceremony last May and registered for china at Macy's. They have been together ten years.

You could clearly hear Letourneau imbuing her student with power; trying to convince the public as she'd convinced herself that Fualaau—her lover, her hero—was on more than equal footing with her: "He dominated me in the most masculine way that any man, any leader, could do."

He was twelve. She was thirty-four.

When Diane DeMartini-Scully first started going for walks with her daughter's fifteen-year-old boyfriend on the North Fork of Long Island, it made him feel special. "She would just talk to me about life situations and shit," he says now, a year and a half later. "It was pretty cool." This is something DeMartini-Scully, a forty-five-year-old blonde who vaguely resembles Erica Jong, would have been good at. She was, until recently, a school psychologist at East Hampton Middle School. She knew how to draw a kid out.

And the boy, let's call him Jason, had some things on his mind. "I was making a lot of money in New York," he says, and when I ask him how, he gives a nervous laugh. "I was doing a lot of things." I ask if the things he was doing and the company he was keeping (mostly in Jamaica, Queens, he says) were part of the reason his family left Mattituck, Long Island, where they lived just down the road from DeMartini-Scully, for Jacksonville, North Carolina, where they currently reside. He says yes, but the reason his mother has given the press for the move was to escape the escalating cost of living on the North Fork. Detective Steven L. Harned of the local Southold Police Department says, "We were already aware of [Jason]. He has had some court cases here on other matters."

When Jason's family was ready to relocate to Jacksonville, he still had a few months of school remaining. It was decided that Jason would finish off the year living at DeMartini-Scully's house on Donna Drive. "We would go to Blockbuster and rent movies, and when we watched them, she would put her hand on my lap," Jason says. "I didn't think much of it at the time."

One night, when DeMartini-Scully's daughter, with whom Jason was still involved, was at a friend's house, and after DeMartini-Scully's son had gone to sleep, she asked Jason if he wanted to watch television with her in her bed. "Then she kissed me."

That night, Jason and DeMartini-Scully "basically did everything." He remembers the experience as "okay...I wouldn't say it was upsetting. I wouldn't say I didn't want to, but...I figured she was letting me stay at her house, I'd just do what she wanted."

This was not an isolated incident. For the next three and a half months, Jason estimates, the two continued having sex at the house and in her car. "Nobody suspected anything," he says. "And I didn't want nobody to know because I was messing around with her daughter. I found it funny that Diane was letting me stay at her house when she knew about that, but I never asked her why: I figured she was doing it because she wanted something."

I ask Jason what he wanted: whether he was having sex with DeMartini-Scully because he enjoyed it or because he felt obliged to. "When I wasn't drunk, I felt pressured to, but when I was drunk, I wanted to...you know what I mean?" He claimed he got alcohol, and sometimes pot, from DeMartini-Scully.

When summer came, DeMartini-Scully took her son and daughter and Jason down to Florida, where they met up with Jason's family for a vacation en route to Jacksonville. What was supposed to be a quick stop to see Jason's family's new house became an extended stay when DeMartini-Scully was injured in an accident. "She hurt her leg pretty bad when I was teaching her how to ride the dirt bike," Jason says. "You could see her bone and shit." She stayed in North Carolina for a month.

When she finally left, Jason's mother was glad to be rid of DeMartini-Scully. She had become suspicious when she found out that Jason and DeMartini-Scully had been in a room with the door locked. But on Columbus Day weekend, unbeknownst to Jason's mother, DeMartini-Scully returned to a hotel in Jacksonville to visit Jason. "So I want to know, what's so special about me?" Jason says. I ask him what he thinks. He laughs. "I'm not gonna say."

He spent three days at the hotel. His mother found out about the visit, and "that's when all the drama started." She contacted the police, who charged DeMartini-Scully with kidnapping and providing marijuana to a minor but not with sexual assault, because Jason had, at this point, already turned sixteen and passed the legal age of consent in North Carolina. She was subsequently charged with third-degree rape and performing a criminal sexual act in Suffolk County, where the age of consent is seventeen.

Jason stayed in school for just three weeks in Jacksonville before he dropped out. He says he will join the Marines after he gets his GED, "but just for the money." He doesn't miss DeMartini-Scully, he says, who by the end was suggesting she wanted to marry him. But he also says he doesn't feel raped. "I just, I don't know, I feel weird. She was thirty years older than me, so I feel a little bit taken advantage of. If I was a girl, I probably wouldn't talk to you about it, but a female can't really rape a guy, you know?"

Jason says he would not have given a statement to the Long Island police incriminating DeMartini-Scully if he hadn't been under pressure. "They said if I didn't they were gonna press charges on me because I was with Diane's daughter," who is only fourteen, and now Jason is seventeen, thus making him guilty of "sexual misconduct" himself. As of his last birthday, Jason's relationships switched status in the eyes of the law: Sex with the then-forty-four-year-old school psychologist who had been after him since he was sixteen became okay; sex with her teenage daughter became a crime.

("It is a strange law," says Harned. "I didn't write them, I just enforce them." Harned says that it is still likely that the Southold Police Department will press charges against Jason for his relationship with the daughter and that Jason was not pushed into giving a statement about the mother.)

"I just think about how Diane's daughter must feel now," Jason says. "I was pretty close to her; I still am. I'm talking to her on the computer right now."

I ask Jason if this is an experience he will try to avoid in the future, getting involved with much older women. He thinks about it for a minute. "Depends how old," he concludes. "How old are you?"

Stalking the Stalkers
Kelly Kyrik

It's late on a Tuesday night and Sarah Kinsler [not her real name], a forty-four-year-old mother of two, is online again.

The former homemaker is not cruising eBay looking for specialty cookware or checking out the latest in designer drapery. Instead she's hard at work in her cramped office, playing the part of a thirteen-year-old girl while chatting with a virtual stranger—one who appears to have all the makings of a pedophile.

Although they've only been Instant Messaging for a few minutes, he's already checked out her profile and declared her "hot," at least judging by the grainy Polaroid shot that Kinsler has posted, which shows an apple-cheeked teen smiling innocently for the camera. He also knows her hobbies— "ditching school, hanging with my friends, and jacking cigs from my mom!"—and her supposed age, but that hasn't deterred him in the least.

"Do u like older guys?" he asks, sending a virtual wink along with his message.

"Dunno…" Kinsler types, hedging a little, as a young teen might. "Maybe, I guess. A/S/L?"

Kinsler, who has ten years' experience trolling for predators, first as a civilian, now as a Reserve officer in a small town in the Bible Belt, uses chatroom lingo to ask her wannabe predator for his Age/Sex/Location. She already knows the answers because she's read his profile, which lists "lots of sex" and "loving pretty girls" as his hobbies. But she wants to draw him out and pin him down, all the while collecting evidence for her chat log.

"All male/Chicago/and that depends," types her wannabe predator, adding a smiley face at the end of his sentence. "How old is too old?" Kinsler sips her tea as the familiar script unfolds, all too aware that she has another live one on her virtual line.

"Gosh," she types, all innocence, "maybe 25?"

"Uh-oh!" he replies, sending a frowny face to show his supposed chagrin along with another wink that reveals his real intentions. "I'm 28, r u gonna ditch me now?"

From experience, Kinsler knows that he's probably ten or so years older than his purported age and already she can tell that there's a good chance that she'll bust this guy, if not tonight, then sometime in the near future. She can also pretty much script how their "relationship" will develop over the course of the next days or weeks.

"After a while he'll start asking questions about my sexuality, or lack thereof," she says. "He'll want to know if I'm a virgin or if I've ever experimented with sex. He'll kind of fish for information to see how sexual I'm willing to be or how far I might go."

Soon, he'll press Kinsler for pictures, maybe ask for a provocative pose. When he asks for phone contact, she'll feign worry that she might get caught to throw him off. Of course, she'll give in at some point and they'll exchange brief, whispered conversations wherein he will press for phone sex while Kinsler giggles and evades his graphic questions. Eventually, if all goes according to plan, he'll start pestering her for a face-to-face meeting. When she finally agrees, he'll probably show up at their prearranged meeting place armed and ready for sex, likely carrying condoms, lubricant, sex toys, and maybe even alcohol and/or drugs.

"Once we've arrested him and have his computer," says Kinsler, a veteran who's seen close to a hundred of "her" offenders convicted, "there will be even more incriminating evidence. He'll usually have a ton of child porn plus chat logs that detail all his online activity, and often there will be evidence of prior victims. These guys almost always plead guilty before trial because there's just no way they can explain away the fact that they're obviously soliciting kids for sex."

But all that comes later. For now, Kinsler waits to see how far this guy is going to go, settling in with a fresh cup of herbal tea and steeling herself for what could be a long night.

Internet Facilitated Crimes

Kinsler isn't the only cop working online to catch pedophiles. As a matter of fact, she's part of a new breed of investigators who are tracking a relatively new crime: Computer Facilitated Crimes Against Children. Hundreds if not thousands of officers are blazing a trail that was virtually unheard of ten years ago, when access to the Internet was limited. Working in conjunction with various organizations like the federally funded Internet Crimes Against Children Task Force (ICAC) and the National Center for Missing and Exploited Children (NCMEC), these new cyber-cops are ferreting out and apprehending pedophiles in chat rooms around the world, which are prime feeding grounds for perverts.

"Pedophiles go where the kids are," says Kinsler, "and since teens spend so much of their time online, these guys just lie in wait in the chatrooms. Every time I log on, even though I'm just sitting there not saying anything, I'm inundated with personal messages from guys. And a lot of them come on really strong right from the start."

The reason for the aggressive and often seemingly reckless behavior of these pedophiles is due in large part to the anonymity of the Internet. Back in the old days, when predators were forced to solicit their victims in real time, it was much harder to meet, talk with, and seduce their intended victims. But now they have the freedom to access, converse with, and groom their prey, and they're able to hone their skills over time. And while pedophiles have of course always been around, many investigators believe that the Internet has brought about a whole new era of abuse.

"My opinion is that the Internet and all the stimuli from child pornography has resulted in an upsurge of victimization," asserts John Schneider [not his real name], an investigator with a large, metropolitan police department located in the western United States. "Before, people were only able to fantasize to a few pictures, and even those were hard to come by. But now with the click of a mouse you can look at thousands of images. These guys simply can't handle all that stimulation and are now going after kids more than they would have in the past."

There's no doubt that the Internet acts as a conduit between perpetrator and victim, and unfortunately, predators often move at lightning speed.

"It doesn't take long to initially hook a couple of potential prospects," says Schneider. "And then once you actually hook up with somebody, depending on how motivated he is, it's usually over quickly. I've had some guys come down to meet us in just two hours."

Predator Typology

Pedophiles who set up meetings with their victims are known as "travelers," and investigators consider them particularly dangerous. Not only are they brazen enough to single-mindedly pursue their prey until they've achieved the ultimate goal—sex with an underage child—once they've started, they rarely stop on their own. An upcoming study of incarcerated travelers reveals that nine out of ten travelers admit to having sexually molested other children before their arrest.

"Some of these offenders are the most dangerous persons a child can meet online," writes Detective James McLaughlin in a report detailing the findings. "One [of the offenders we apprehended] would operate concurrently in teen sex rooms and child torture rooms. He eventually sent money in the mail to get a male child to run away. One other offender's home was searched and photographs of dead children in shallow graves were seized. Still another was already in custody for child homicide. The subpoena had been complied with and the account owner/suspect identified, but it was too late."

The Keene study also details three other types of predators:

"Collectors," as their name implies, collect and trade child porn, and they dedicate extreme amounts of time and energy to their particular predilection. It's not unusual for a collector to have thousands or even tens of thousands of images on his hard drive, usually organized into very specific categories. McLaughlin refers to collectors as "entry-level" offenders, given their lack of previous crimes and the fact that they don't come into personal contact with victims.

"Chatters" also typically do not meet their victims. They do, however, spend an inordinate amount of time cruising chatrooms in search of potential prey. According to the report, they often offer themselves up as advisors and are only too happy to talk about all things sexual. They're usually interested in cybersex and will often graduate to phone sex, although in general they have no desire to meet a real child in person."

"Manufacturers," however—those who are involved in the actual manufacturing and distribution of child porn—are usually involved personally with their victims. While some choose to clandestinely photograph children at public places, restrooms, and changing rooms, many have actual hands-on experience. This particular type of abuser is considered every bit as dangerous as the traveler, especially because, as the Keene investigation revealed, many of these pedophiles photographed "children they molested years ago, were actively molesting, or were in the process of seducing."

Pedophile Profiles

Perhaps the most dangerous thing about these new Internet predators, however, is that they are not always who they seem; these guys often don't look or act like the stereotypically sleazy pedophile. Certainly most of them are socially isolated and considered odd or weird by their peers or coworkers, but just as many are as "normal" as the guy next door. They're fathers and soccer coaches and teachers and councilmen and lawyers and even priests.

"We caught someone recently," says Robert Hanlon, Chief of Police in a Midwest suburb, "and you'd have thought he was the last person who could molest a child. He'd been the youth minister in church and wrote articles about family and love and kids." [Real name and location changed]

There are some general similarities, however. The vast majority (an estimated 99 percent) of Internet predators are male and typically in their thirties, although there are, of course, plenty of teens and elderly men who have been arrested. These men are predominantly white but come from all classes of life, from the unemployed to laborers to CEOs. And these are not innocent guys who accidentally stumble into a trap while surfing the Internet looking for some fun; they are actively pursuing a sexual relationship with an underage girl.

"We arrested a guy recently who came down from somewhere in Ventura County," says Detective Darin Lenyi of the Laguna Beach, California, Police Department, "and he never once questioned our age. We clearly told him we were fourteen, we even have a profile that states that we're fourteen and in the eighth grade. Plus we come off as naïve on all different kinds of subjects. We're extremely nervous when it comes to wanting to have sex and getting pregnant. For example, they talk about oral sex, and we ask if it's possible to get pregnant that way."

To boost conviction rates (which typically run 100 percent) and avoid entrapment, most investigators continually remind the perpetrator of their age and innocence, but these offenders plow ahead anyway. Many officers describe these predators' behavior as addictive and obsessive in nature, and say they hunt down their prey—lonely young girls or boys—with a surprising fervor.

"They just can't think beyond getting to that kid," says Kinsler. "They will give up their jobs, their salaries, their homes, everything. They just don't care. It's like it's stronger than drugs. They're just addicted."

Internet predators use several different strategies to attract their victims. Some alternate sexual aggression with tenderness in a ploy reminiscent of the good cop/bad cop concept. Others imply remorse and ask for their would-be victim's forgiveness, alternating their requests for pity with sly seduction. Some present themselves as a mentor or a teacher, others come off as a close friend. Many feed on the division between adolescents and parents. "I bet your parents don't understand you," they tell their victims, "but I do, and I'll always listen to you. You can talk to me about anything." Almost all of them play on the insecurities of those in the throes of early teenage angst, a demographic that is particularly vulnerable to the attentions of a virtual stranger.

"It's always the same scenario," says Hanlon. "These girls are in their early teens and they desperately want to be liked. They want to be loved. Sometimes they're sheltered, they're not really attuned to what life is all about. And a lot of them have never been told that they're pretty or that they're sexy. They just eat it up."

Unfortunately, most of these crimes, whether virtual or in person, manage to fly under the radar. While there are no firm statistics as to how many kids are victimized, most investigators believe that they apprehend less than one percent of those that are committing these crimes.

"The bottom line is that it's an underreported deal," says Schneider, "because the last things these kids are going to do is tell their parents that they made a mistake, that they talked to someone and then went and met them for sex. As a matter of fact, in the majority of cases we only find out about it when the kids get caught sneaking out of or back into the house, or, in one case we had, when they just don't come home at all."

Investigators agree that parents, a teen's first line of defense against predators, are woefully ignorant about the dangers online, especially when it comes to chatrooms. These parents aren't aware that of the thirty-five million teens online, one in five has been propositioned, with a third of those come-ons considered aggressive, and that predators now have 24/7 access to children right in their very own bedrooms. Also, they're often in denial about the fact their kids may be participating in this kind of activity; chatting with people they don't know, people who may be out to hurt them.

"Parents just don't think it's going to happen to their child," says Schneider, "and they either don't have parental blocks or don't know that their kids can get online with no restrictions at their friends' houses. And they don't realize that since kids feel safe at home, they're more bold when they're online, especially because it's not a face-to-face thing. I mean, they have webcams at sleepovers. They play games like Truth or Dare."

With needy children online and their parents absent or ignorant, undercover online investigators are left as the last line of defense in protecting teens against pedophiles. More and more officers are being trained in the fine art of apprehending predators online, and a total of forty-six states now have an ICAC Task Force. But the field is still woefully underpopulated. One investigator in Colorado estimates that there are only eight officers, mostly working part-time, in the entire state. But those that are scouting the information superhighway for pedophiles are dedicated.

"If the police don't do anything, who will?" asks Hanlon. "Who's going to stand between the kids and the predators? It's unfortunate in our society, but parents aren't necessarily doing their jobs. So if we officers don't do it, I'm afraid that we're going to lose our children."

Kinsler, who has dedicated her life to protecting children, spends upward of thirty hours online a week tracking pedophiles, traveling to her office at all hours of the day and night to chat online and talk on the phone with the offenders. But despite the fact that she's dealing with the scourge of society and has to communicate on an intimate level with offenders and their often violent or manipulative sexual fantasies, she tries to put her work and the often horrifying images and words in perspective.

"As long as he's talking to me," she says, with a shrug, "I know he's not talking to a real kid."

Sex in Iran
Pari Esfandiari
and Richard Buskin

The film begins with a dark-haired man in his mid-twenties lying naked on a bed, hands behind his head, casually enjoying sex. Reaching out, he takes hold of the camera and swings it around to reveal the attractive brunette who's on top of him. About the same age and wearing nothing but a smile, she rides him, coolly allowing a creaking twin bed to make all the noise within the red-hued confines of the small, dimly lit room. The pleasure on her face is unmistakable and, to many in the strict Islamic country of Iran, so is the face itself.

Zahra Amir Ebrahimi is one of that nation's most ascendant actresses, known for portraying religious, morally upstanding characters on a trio of the past few years' top-rated TV soaps: "Help Me," "Strangeness" and, most famously, "Narges," a prince-and-the-pauper-type drama about the trials and tribulations of a wealthy patriarch's three children, which was watched by 68 percent of the

Iranian audience during its run. Now here she allegedly is, both dominant and submissive, on a twenty-six-minute-and-seventeen-second recording, giving a performance that's causing a storm in her homeland. Nicknamed *Narges 2,* the film seems to depict three encounters of tender lovemaking involving scenes of leisurely fore-play, fellatio, and ejaculation. Though dimly lit and photographed with a not always advantageously positioned camera, the home movie is burning up the Internet, and a DVD has sold an estimated one hundred thousand copies and grossed about four million dollars—a record in the annals of Iranian moviemaking—since the story broke last October. But all may not be as it seems, at least according to Ebrahimi.

Dubbed Iran's Paris Hilton and interrogated multiple times at the request of Tehran's hard-line chief prosecutor, Saeed Mortazavi, Ebrahimi strenuously denies participating in the sex tape, which her ex-partner and costar has reportedly claimed they filmed at her apartment a couple of years ago. Instead she insists the man authorities call Mr. X—identified by our sources as Shahram Sha-hamat, an aspiring film director—employed a look-alike actress and professional montage techniques to create a fake video in order to ruin Ebrahimi's career after she jilted him because of his infidel-ity. If her story is true, he did a pretty convincing job. If not, she could be in real trouble. Were she convicted of violating morality laws, Ebrahimi would face the possibility of a public lashing with a leather strap, jail time, or worse.

Initially rumored by the Iranian media to have committed sui-cide while in police custody, Ebrahimi has been barred by authori-ties from speaking publicly. However, she made a statement to the Iranian Labor News Agency in November 2006, saying in a sar-castic tone, "I wish to reassure or at least inform my friends that I, Zahra Ebrahimi, the so-called actress who looks very much like the one who appears in the movie that's been exchanging hands since the middle of Ramadan, am in good health, and as yet I haven't found enough reason to kill myself." Whatever the truth, Ebrahimi has had the ironic experience of becoming a fixture on the front pages of several of the independent but tightly controlled daily papers (on state-run TV and radio the story got minimal play) while watching her career go down the tubes. Although "Narges" was on hiatus when the scandal broke, release of her two most recent movies, *A Trip to Heidaloo* and *It's a Star,* has been delayed on the advice of authorities while the investigation continues. Since she hasn't been charged, no ban has been ordered, but in Iran it would be more than a little foolish to ignore such advice. Within a year of the 1979 revolution that saw the Ayatollah Khomeini overthrow the Shah's government, Iran was converted from the region's most Westernized society into a restrictive Islamic republic. For many this amounted to a hijacking—the democratically chosen replacement for a royal despot transformed the country into a hard-line theocracy. The subsequent mass migration, coupled with the countless executions of activists and deposed power brokers labeled *mofsed e fel arz*—the most corrupt on earth—left behind a population composed of people who either supported the government or were too exhausted to resist, all of whom were expected to reject Western values in favor of strict Islamic law. Once the government realized this was impossible to enforce, it settled for public obeisance to morality laws and focused on raising a new generation that would passionately embrace the regime.

It was targeting a large group. Iran is now home to around seventy million people, but because of mass fatalities in the war with Iraq in the 1980s and an officially sanctioned baby boom, the country has a median age of twenty-five, one of the world's youngest. Yet despite the government's indoctrination, it appears that many young Iranians have rejected traditional beliefs. The Ebrahimi scandal provides us with a window into the psyche of people who quite simply have developed their own philosophical outlook: live now, and let the future take care of itself. More important, the *Narges 2* video exposes the double standards within Iranian culture that toy with Islamic rules, lifting the veil on a schizoid society that juxtaposes religious fundamentalism with a youthful lust for sex, drink, drugs, parties, and material possessions. The very idea that Ebrahimi could have been a willing participant flies in the face of her prior public image, and it also gets in the face of a society torn between tradition and modernity, unsure of its identity, and ambivalent about moral values and social norms. Regardless of country or jurisdiction, there are legal repercussions whenever a personal sex tape is made public without all the participants' consent. However, in Iran a person can be in trouble just for having made the film. Westerners can generally do what they want in private, but in the Islamic world each person has a moral duty to publicly acknowledge his or her transgressions. And since religion underpins the society, moral obligations have become legal ones, too.

In Iran, sharia law governs everyone's life, private and public. Islam differs from other religions that discourage nonprocreative sex by acknowledging a man's sex drive, though it ignores a woman's. This has resulted in a culture that allows men to gratify themselves but expects women to be submissive. But with Ebrahimi or Madame X clearly enjoying herself, the sexual role of Iranian women is being redefined—or will be if authorities don't clamp down soon. Camcorders weren't around when sharia law was conceived, and now it is trying to play catch-up amid a torrent of vivid images and divided opinions. No one is quite sure where to draw the line.

"These DVDs are targeting our youths and endangering family morals," declared a letter from 150 members of the Iranian

Parliament to Ayatollah Hashemi Shahroudi, the country's judiciary chief. "The government should accelerate the process of arrest and conviction and then hand out the harshest penalties." The letter called for those who produce and distribute sex films to be punished by hanging. In response, acclaimed writer and political activist Emadeddin Baghi wrote an open letter to Parliament, calling for moderation. "Execution will resolve nothing," he asserted, pointing out that excising the root of the problem should be the primary concern. "The question to be asked is why this immoral DVD has broken Iranian film-industry records by making four million dollars. That figure shows the extent of our social problems." Among those problems is prostitution, particularly teenage prostitution. The reputable Iranian Labor News Agency has estimated the number of prostitutes to be between 300,000 and 600,000, and the proposed remedies diverge just as widely. One female parliamentarian called for public hangings of prostitutes, while several prominent clerics suggested legalizing brothels. This stimulated a national debate, with the government vowing to address the root causes, which it identified as poverty, unemployment, drug addiction, and family conflicts. It also recognized that men marrying later and the increasing divorce rate have left more single males around to drive up demand. But condemning prostitution and porn is easy for the authorities.

It's another matter to deal with the titillating image of a naked actress with a Brazilian wax enjoying sex in multiple positions. Ignoring it could be perceived as legal approval; punishing it could open a can of worms—try enforcing a ban on all such behavior at a time when more and more people are filming their own sex sessions. Even with several months having passed since the sex-tape story broke, simply raising the incident in any cafe or shopping area is enough to illustrate its impact. Just as the O.J. Simpson case gave Americans a way to discuss and confront their feelings about such difficult subjects as race, sex, and police power, the Ebrahimi scandal is allowing Iranians to confront their attitudes about sex and construct rationales for accepting or not accepting what they've seen. We spoke to a variety of urban, middle-class Iranians, and though we received a range of reactions, none were condemnatory. Some even found the film exciting. "My husband, Mani, and I watched the film without feeling guilty," says Yasmin. (Fearing government retribution for publicly expressing their opinions, those interviewed for this article have asked that their surnames be withheld.) "Personally I don't care if it was Ebrahimi or if she was drugged. We watched it as a porno movie. The sex was hot. I kept saying, 'What great love.' My husband kept saying, 'What great sex.' Watching this kind of movie isn't a sin."

Curiosity drew Pejman, a high school teacher, to the film. "My primary reason for watching it was to see how much naked sex Ebrahimi has in the movie," he admits. "I always liked her in 'Narges,' and I think she is very pretty. I also wanted to see if it was really her."

Even conservative Iranians have seen the film. Mehri, a thirty-year-old Tehran woman who describes herself as very traditional, watched the film just to confirm what her husband had described taking place. "That she did something sacrilegious and immoral makes me very angry at her," she says, "but the fact that her reputation has been forever destroyed makes me feel very sorry for her." Behnam, a young graduate student at the University of Tehran, watched the "supermovie," as Iranians often refer to porn flicks, with nine fellows in his dormitory. Each chipped in around four dollars to buy the DVD—at one time the going rate was as high as fifty dollars, equivalent to the average weekly wage in Iran. "Most of the guys saw the film at least a couple of times," Behnam says.

"Once to check if it was really her and then to actually enjoy what was going on. Afterward the dorm walls were covered with Zahra Ebrahimi's pictures, some torn from magazines of her wearing a veil and others nude screen grabs from the movie."

Behnam says he did not enjoy the film. "I couldn't watch it all the way through," he says. "I got sick during the part where the guy forces her to have sex from behind and she cries. Clearly she is unhappy. I thought it was inhuman." Most who have seen the film would say Behnam is misreading the scene. Ebrahimi seems to be shedding tears of emotion, not pain; she writhes sensuously and caresses her lover with apparent affection. Even so, we often see what we want to see. Behnam's interpretation is typical of this conflicted society, where people move unpredictably between traditional thoughts and modern behavior, and modern thoughts and traditional behavior, and where it may be easier to feel sorry for Zahra the victim than accept the sight of a liberated woman enjoying sex.

Although President Mahmoud Ahmadinejad's ultraconservative government constantly decries the corrupting effects of Western culture, it can do little to control people's private actions. Consequently, it has sought to make an example of the highest-profile offenders, even when the crime is less than salacious. For instance, a TV host was recently fired for being filmed dancing with the bride at a wedding. Perhaps because the government is unsure about how to deal with immoral personal behavior, it has shifted its focus toward those who publicly distribute the depiction. An aboveground porn industry doesn't exist in Iran, but in this era of camcorders and the Internet, amateur porn has flourished. Voyeurism is big; government-approved intrusiveness and a general awareness of people's double lives make snooping a habit, if not a guilty pleasure. People's appetites were initially fulfilled by the curious distribution of home movies showing ordinary citizens' parties and family gatherings. Circulated next were videos of celebrities attending illegal mixed-gender gatherings where alcohol was served, as well as photos of the unveiled faces of actresses. Next, more flesh was exposed on film; women in swimsuits were photographed, sometimes with hidden cameras and cell phones. Before long, the movies grew more daring. Men secretly filmed their girlfriends in their bedrooms, though not necessarily naked or having sex; just being there with a man and without a veil was shocking enough. Sometimes the images were used to blackmail the women, causing scandal and disgrace. Three years ago a film appeared on the Internet showing thirteen high school girls wearing Western-style clothes and dancing without veils at a birthday party. Fearing their parents' reaction, all thirteen committed suicide. Soon after, a man in the northern city of Ray beat his daughter to death when he thought he recognized her wearing "revealing" clothes and partying with Iranian soccer players in some footage. He was mistaken and was sentenced to three years in jail. Finally the first overtly sexy film of willing participants began to circulate. A group of young women from the southern city of Ahvaz danced and stripped in front of the camera, a kind of Iranian *Girls Gone Wild* that did big business. Then came *Narges 2,* the first homegrown sex movie to allegedly feature a well-known personality. Given the low overhead of DVD replication, it earned those who distributed it a fortune—as well as a possible death sentence. Seven entrepreneurs are currently awaiting their fate behind bars, but many others have jumped into the market; as a result the film can be found in street bazaars, car trunks and, most helpfully, the hands of home-delivery merchants. Among these *filmei,* as the latter are commonly known, is one Mr. Farhang, whose name evidently reflects his sensibilities, since it translates into English as Mr. Culture.

"Getting home delivery isn't all that easy," he says. "You must be referred by someone the supplier already knows, and then initial contact should be by phone in order to establish trust. Eighty to eighty-five percent of my clients demand porn material from me, and these are mostly wealthy men, although in the case of the Ebrahimi movie, women have also been interested in seeing an actress display her femininity within a private space. This is a growing industry." And in response, the government has become more threatening. "Beforehand, if we were arrested, we'd be thrown in jail and would have to pay a fine," he says. "But now things are more dangerous. I'm frightened."

The Iranian people have grown quite adept at maintaining appearances. As long as a woman wears a *hijab*, her inner beliefs are her own. The facade is all that counts, and the result is that during the past twenty-eight years two very different lifestyles have existed side by side. A walk on the streets of Tehran suggests a population governed by strict religious and moral values. This is also the image projected overseas. Move just outside the city center, however, and you'll find women undermining the government's authority by wearing heavy makeup and reducing their *hijabs* to fashionably tight, sexy outfits. On many you'll see nose bandages, betraying an appetite for cosmetic surgery. And behind closed doors, there's even greater deviation. In the eyes of many Iranians, the only change wrought upon them by the Islamic revolution is that once they prayed in private and partied in public and now it's the other way around.

It is a Thursday night in the summer of 2005, the Saturday-like height of the Islamic weekend. A party is taking place in Shahrak Gharb, a neighborhood in northwest Tehran, at a large white mansion owned by a businessman who made a fortune importing machine parts in the years following the revolution. The house is typical of the area—modern yet unpretentious from the outside. Guests have been asked to deflect official attention by staggering their arrival and coming by taxi or not parking too close to the house. Most in attendance are in their thirties or older, couples, some married, all affluent. Or at least they seem that way, dressed in designer clothes, the women dripping in jewelry under the mandatory long coats they wear with head scarves that they remove the second they enter the house. This is standard practice for any party or get-together in Iran, as is the need to keep the coats and scarves close at hand in case of a police raid. Also handy are wet-wipe tissues for makeup removal, as well as chewing gum and breath spray to mask the smell of alcohol.

A police raid tonight, however, is unlikely. The host has already paid a police officer not only to be incurious but to provide all the liquor. Not a bad deal.

The drinks are in the kitchen, hidden in a cupboard and served in plastic cups that can easily be ditched should a uniformed cop drop by. Soft drinks and snacks are being served by a team of maids in the main room, where people are talking and mingling, and in the rooms en suite, where some are dancing to both Arabic and Iranian pop music—with the appropriate moves for each—and listening to an assortment of English and American hits. Next door is the obligatory opium room. People sit on velvet floor cushions next to small tables with dates and other sweet snacks and pass the pipe; smoke rises as poetry is read and mellow Iranian classical music is played. Among the guests is Catayon, a forty-two-year-old homemaker with an open attitude toward sex. Her husband, Iraj, has another wife, which isn't outrageous in a society where up to four are allowed, along with a string of lovers, which is also less than remarkable for a wealthy man. At least Catayon feels entitled to take lovers of her own. "I knew before we arrived that Iraj had been trying to get close to Mitra, a friend whose marriage is going through a rocky time because her husband spent a weekend with my half sister," Catayon later recalls. "As soon as we got to the party, he poured Mitra a drink and began talking with her. That was fine—it gave me the opportunity to chat with Kamshad, whom I had always fancied. Since Kamshad's wife was spending the summer in the United States, I could have him to myself. We both knew it wouldn't be long before Iraj and Mitra would disappear into one of the upstairs bedrooms, and at that point we could find a quiet corner."

This kind of scene, although not commonplace, serves as a counterpoint to the fundamentalist extreme often portrayed as the norm to the outside world. There's a widespread misconception in the West that sex outside marriage is illegal in Iran, but in fact Islam permits sex outside marriage as long as it is conducted within a legal framework known as *seigheh.* This is a temporary contract between a man and a woman that allows sexual interaction and sets conditions including the financial obligations of the parties and the actual duration, which can range from a few hours to many years.

This controversial practice, which dates back to the beginning of Islam, lost its popularity in modern Iran until the revolution, when it passed into law. Since then it has commonly been employed by young couples avoiding government harassment, poor or divorced women seeking protection and financial support, and others. Though widely regarded as a loophole legalizing prostitution, *seigheh* could be another way of exonerating Zahra Amir Ebrahimi should matters proceed to that extent. It may seem surprising that religious hard-liners would allow such a spongy exception, but those crusty-looking mullahs and ayatollahs aren't nearly as narrow-minded as many people think. Over the years, several of them have taken it upon themselves to serve as the nation's sexual arbiters. Indeed, for years following the revolution, one of the most popular TV programs in Iran was one viewers called the "Gili Show." Each must-see episode featured the Ayatollah Gilani discoursing on a particular topic, often of a sexual nature, and discussing the rights and wrongs as they pertain to sharia law. Today Iranians use the Internet to hear similar advice from ayatollahs all over the Middle East. For instance, at islamonline.net, a site run by Al-Jazeera Publishing, Iranians can see Qatar-based cleric Sheikh Yusuf al-Qaradawi declare that "Muslim jurists are of the opinion that it is lawful for the husband to perform cunnilingus on his wife or a wife to perform the similar act for her husband, and there is no wrong in doing so. But if sucking leads to releasing semen, then it is *makruh* [blameworthy], although there is no decisive evidence to forbid it." On the same website visitors are cautioned "not to develop any of the medical symptoms that may result from masturbation, such as weak eyesight, a weak nervous system and/or back pain. More important, feelings of guilt and anxiety can be complicated by missing obligatory prayers because of the need to shower after every incidence of masturbation." Thanks to external influences as well as Islam's practicality about the subject, sexual mores have definitely been relaxed.

"In sexual matters, most Iranians take their lead from Iraj Mirza," says Reza, a psychologist, referring to the early twentieth-century poet and intellectual known for his extremely graphic musings on the subject. "His advice was to do it but not talk about it. Well, Iranians' attitudes toward sex are currently evolving. These days, virginity is still an important issue in many towns and villages, where young girls could lose their lives for indulging in illicit sex. Yet for many guys in Tehran the whole issue of a girl's virginity is no longer relevant." Oddly, says Reza, this change may be the unintentional consequence of some government policies. "Years ago boys and girls would date by meeting in parks and other public places. Thanks to the government's harsh regulations, this is no longer possible. The only place they can hook up is behind closed doors, so instead of things progressing slowly, the teens end up in bed faster than ever. On average, teenagers now have sex on their second or third date, and doing so is considered normal among large sections of the nation's youth."

Such changes have taken place in many countries but are happening so rapidly in Iran that the government hasn't had time to plan its next move. A sociocultural revolution heavily influenced by the West is confronting these nations head-on, and those in power find themselves caught between the devil and the deep blue Caspian Sea.

Kayvan knows all about his friend Rozbeh's sex parties. The twenty-four-year-old college student had such a great time at the three he attended that he asked if he could bring his friend Pouya to the next gathering, and Rozbeh agreed. Like Kayvan, Pouya is a rich kid studying computing, but at the age of twenty-two he's never gone to this kind of party before, so he's feeling a bit self-conscious when Rozbeh greets them at the door of his parents' villa in Lavasan, a suburb of northern Tehran, on a warm and sunny evening in the fall of 2006. But Pouya's nerves quickly disappear when Rozbeh, dressed in a fashionably loose sweater and baggy pants, ushers the two young men into a romantically candlelit main room and introduces them to four girls sitting on a leather sofa. All are wearing sexy, tight-fitting tops and jeans, and two other guys are sitting at the bar, drinking wine and vodka.

"The number of men and women should always be equal," says

Rozbeh. He's a computer-studies student from a wealthy family and sports designer stubble and spiky gelled hair. "After all, when people pair up and have sex, we can't have someone left on his or her own." The extent of Pouya's track record in the sack may consist of a couple of times with his girlfriend, yet he isn't shy. On this particular evening he's not all that choosy about whom he'll end up with. "It's just one night," he reasons, "and afterward we'll never meet again." All things being equal, though, he'd rather have a girl younger than he is, someone less experienced. Like most of his fellow countrymen, he would prefer to save face than learn something new.

Seven couples have been invited to the party, and when Rozbeh puts on a heavy-metal album they all start dancing on cue. Keenly aware of needing to escape police attention, the host avoids cranking up the volume. Often, dancing lasts several hours, but it's hardly the key item on tonight's agenda. It's true that these party animals are from rich and middle-class backgrounds, and that they belong to a faster crowd than most kids do. But it's also true that they are pacesetters. Other young people may not be as daring, but they're also image conscious and interested in fun; in that way they too challenge authority and pose a threat to the government.

Though sex may be discussed on television, it's usually a verboten subject in the average Iranian home. Pouya's parents have no idea how he spends his time, or they choose to have no idea as long as he's not overly involved in politics. "My going to university makes them very comfortable," he says, "and they don't give much thought to who I'm seeing or what I'm doing." Indeed, college provides kids with a no-questions-asked safety net, which may be why the Department of Education recently warned families about the rapidly increasing level of drug use among students. Still, there are protocols. "No one does drugs at sex parties," Kayvan insists. "If they do drugs before coming to the party, that's another matter. Sex parties are different from X parties"—ecstasy-fueled raves—"where you can find everything from grass to crack. At sex parties there's just drink to help people lose their inhibitions."

They may lose their inhibitions, but they don't totally misplace them. Compatibility and confidentiality remain keys to a good time. Couples generally require their own rooms, meaning that even in larger homes, guest lists never exceed twenty people. Group sex and switching partners are virtually unknown. "I've never seen group sex," says Farshad, one of the other male guests. "At the end of the night, when everyone's totally drunk, people may fall on top of one other and play around, but I've never seen it lead to very much. Group sex is for the movies. As far as I'm concerned, the girl I sleep with at a party is mine until the night is over. We are, after all, Iranians, and there's something in our psyche that precludes certain kinds of behavior." The relationships end with the night.

"That's the rule," says Kayvan, "and you can be sure that if I'm invited to Rozbeh's next sex party, I won't meet the girls who were here tonight. We don't enjoy being recognized, and it's also more fun to sleep with someone when you know nothing of her past or future. Instead, for a few hours you can just focus on the moment." Still, why do these young men risk arrest? It's not for sex; after all, the government allows *seigheh*. What the government is against is pure fun, and this is what the young people are flouting. "People need to have fun," Kayvan says. "Leisure time is all about going to parties and having drink, drugs, and even sex with a girl. It's about *hal*—enjoying yourself to the fullest. And it's the same for girls. They enjoy having sex too, and they want it. Of course, for five thousand to six thousand toman [five to six dollars] I can have sex with a prostitute, but sex isn't what it's all about. It's about partying, dancing to heavy-metal music, being with friends and plenty of *hal.*" These days, *hal* is the mantra of the young, while that of their parents is "See no evil, hear no evil." This, after all, is a country of pretense: while the government pretends it doesn't know about its citizens' private transgressions, the parents pretend they don't know the extent of their children's double lives, and the offspring pretend they're obeying the rules—up to a point. "I've been arrested a number of times," says Leila, a twenty-three-year-old coed at yet another covert party in the Tehran suburbs. At this one there's only dancing and drinking, which means all present are taking a huge risk to have what a vast portion of the world regards as fun. "The first time, I was frightened, but after that I didn't care. It's always the same: The police are rude, they push us around, and then they take us to an overnight prison where they question us and give us advice. Maybe they slap some of the guys in the face. They're such idiots." Since the arrests aren't a big deal to Leila, she acts with little sense of fear or shame. "The government is an irrelevant nuisance," she shrugs. "My father has to pay a one hundred thousand toman fine [one hundred dollars] every time I'm arrested."

"So what?" interjects her friend Sahar.

"Our parents wanted the revolution. Let them pay!"

Skeptical of promises of an afterlife, fed up with social restrictions, and bearing the brunt of the country's chronic unemployment, Iranian youths are well aware of how their peers live elsewhere in the world. Thanks to satellite TV and the Internet, they see the excitement and opportunities denied to them, and they're angry. They hold their government responsible for the country's lousy economic situation as well as its international isolation. They struggle with a national pride that was badly bruised when reformist former president Mohammad Khatami's hopes for a "dialogue among civilizations" evaporated when President Bush named Iran to the "axis of evil" in 2002. That was soon followed by the election of anti-American populist Ahmadinejad to the presidency. He promised to restore that pride, create more jobs, and fight corruption. To date, little of this has been realized, leaving young people feeling trapped with no way forward, betrayed by and ambivalent toward a West whose freedom and fashions they invariably try to emulate.

That's why many among this generation of educated and intelligent young people choose to live in the moment, justifying their party lifestyle as resistance to the authorities, as a cry for democracy. In response the government has displayed a little more tolerance toward their Western-inspired activities and pro-Western attitudes. Call it a compromised democracy, one that enables people to speak effectively through their vote for parliamentarians and the president while ceding ultimate control to an unelected, all-powerful supreme leader.

As a nation, Iran is wary of the interference of foreign powers. During the twentieth century, the country's path to democracy was often thwarted by the goals of great powers, the United States included, and by homegrown authoritarians who seized power in the name of social progress and national security. Today the country feels threatened again. If the current nuclear dispute serves as a pretext for the West to impose sanctions or take actions even more drastic, the regime will have all the excuse it needs to strangle civil rights and avert—or at least delay—its own demise. Yet a more open and less confrontational approach would make it more likely that the country can stay on the path to democracy. Last December's local elections showed that few are happy with Ahmadinejad, but that doesn't mean the regime is in danger of collapse, and a hard-line policy out of Washington will only help prop it up. Instead, an approach that invites dialogue and perhaps other inducements is far more likely to persuade authorities to observe human rights and encourage a population that is actually very pro-Western to push for greater freedom. The time is ripe.

The Ebrahimi affair has damaged the government-contrived facade of ubiquitous ultraconservatism, and it's no longer a question of if but when the veil will be lifted on the real Iran. Thanks to an amateur sex video that has delivered a direct hit to the status quo, the government's propaganda has been laid as bare as the lovers on the screen.

Surface Tensions
Jen Cross

After nearly ten years of working actively to be seen and recognized as not just *dyke*, but as *butch*, I've put on a skirt again, and not just because I like how it looks, but because I want someone bigger and more masculine to bend me over, push the skirt above my hips, and fuck me with it still on. Someone like my lover. Someone who, coincidentally or not, is, like my stepfather, also bigger and more masculine than me.

A decade is a long time to shut down the body.

I pass as a white, heterosexual woman, and do not pass as a victim/survivor of sexual abuse. Or maybe it all depends on which direction you're talking: passing "in" to visibly marked identity, or passing "out" of awareness, moving stealthily? Part of passing as a straight woman is not showing her wounds (she won't attract a man that way). No, wait. Straight girls are supposed to show their wounds, are at least supposed to be weaker-than, just not too needy; not so wounded that they can't still take good care of someone else.

Anyway, after not passing (as straight) and passing (as a vaguely masculine dyke) for many years, it has been difficult and painful for me to step back into the mainstream, heterosexual, heteronormative view—to become the seen and unseen thing, the remarked upon and the unmarked/unremarkable, that most abhorred by and pitied by dykes (more so even than straight men): the straight girl. As my lover is a passing butch, we are often read as a straight couple, possibly even by other queers. This peculiar invisibility, juxtaposed all over me with the ostensible safety of hetero-privilege (however questionable that privilege becomes, given that we are an interracial couple), drapes across my shoulders and weighs me down.

When I first came out, I slowly moved from girly-feminine to as masculine as I could make myself without giving up hoop earrings and the occasional night on the town (for the drag ball) in full girl dress. My hair got shorter and shorter, my clothes got boxier. I bought men's shoes, sports bras; longed to rid myself of my breasts and hips, and wanted to become the boyish butch dyke, the passing boy, the *boy*. I loved it when I got called *Sir*, and never got upset when someone was confused at my entering the women's bathroom. I was delighted. I thought I'd accomplished something, had successfully passed as the kind of dyke I so longed to be and thought I was supposed to be.

As for so many others, as far as I was concerned, *dyke* was synonymous with *masculine woman*, which worked just fine for me. As a teenager, the femininity I learned was entirely shaped by my stepfather and his racist, classist sexism (and what sexism isn't racist and classist and more, all informing the others until we're tied together in knots of oppression that shape us, pull us side to side, or side by side?). I wanted to put as much distance as possible between my surviving, queer self and the construction of my stepfather's that (I believed) I'd been. I thought feminine belonged to him. I took off my girlskin. I wanted to slice off all the curves, remove the breasts, take off the ass that he'd touched. This desire just happened to mesh smoothly with the longing to fit in as a dyke.

See, I wanted to pass as *marked*. Moments of recognition, of queer visibility, snared me into my desired sense of self. After my stepfather decided to teach me how porn stars please their men, I learned to hide in plain sight, became the hyper-heterosexual/ super-sexualized smart teenage girl. "Maybe a little eccentric," thought the teachers at school, the acquaintance-friends, the guidance counselors; it never crossed their minds to ask if I was being raped at home nearly every day. During that time, I was invisible in the ways I wanted to be seen, invisible as someone being tortured at home, as a captured child. After coming out (from under him *and* as queer), I wanted to be seen; if I wasn't going to be marked as a survivor by how I looked and moved through the world; by God, I was going to be seen as a dyke, and that meant becoming a butch. I internalized the identity, came out as trans, even, to various people and communities. I got read as a teenage boy or young man now and then and loved it. This was what I understood dykeness to mean; I felt the femmes were frauds, clueless, and, most problematic, *not marked*.

I hoped that homophobia would come to my aid in this scheme of visibility, and wanted, just once, for someone to ask me if my stepfather had "made me this way" when he raped me. Made me gay. Turned me queer. I had all my defiant, indignant, glorious answers ripe and ready, but no one ever asked.

I wanted to believe in my surface and yours, I wanted to be brutally exposed and I wasn't, as it turns out, but I was: every time I walked down the sidewalk, I took for granted a queer visibility that others may or may not have actually perceived. It just wasn't rent from me, that enacted self: I was no threat to anyone. It was a scene. It was something possible, at least, that tension between who I was hidden internally and who I was on my surface.

These days, I no longer pass as gay, unless I'm at a dyke event with my butch lover close by, and even then I don't pass as inherently gay, but gay-by-association. I very often find that my attempts to make eye contact with a stranger who I read as a dyke are misread (as the staring of yet one more confused straight girl?). How many femmes did I ignore/dismiss/remain ignorant of during my first ten years as an out dyke? Now I know.

When I was a boy, even though I still had to actively come out as a survivor, at least I was (I thought) seen as *something*. These days, I have to come out as survivor *and* come out as gay. Now, what's seen first are all the things my stepfather remarked upon, lavished attention upon, built and formulated himself. I want to vomit them off my body sometimes, instead of just battening them down with tight undergarments: breasts, hips, ass, neckline: body. These days, I am again the unhappy recipient of all the trappings and charming indications that I pass as a *female*: smacky kissing sounds from random men, "Nice Big Tits," come-ons, invitations out on dates, eye contact that isn't simply received as *Hello* but as *Let's Go Fuck Right Now*, gazes that stroke across my body, *How You Doin', Baby? Where's Your Man?*

What about the whole incest thing? What does it mean to pass as a survivor? I mean, to be *read* as a survivor? Given that so many of us in this fucking culture have survived some kind of sexual abuse—do we all pass? It's the norm? And still, the experience/identity is silenced, unless you're crying all the time, can't have sex, are unable to be intimate (and who doesn't have intimacy issues in this time of torture, television and target marketing?). If you're relatively functional, forget it. No one wants to talk about survivorhood except your therapist, and she's getting paid.

What does it mean to be marked *survivor* in the same way as we're marked *gender*, or *sexuality, race, class*? Is it possible to wear the identity like clothing? Is it all in the speech, a lingo peppered with words like *triggered* and meetings and group references and self-forgiveness? Would a stranger ever be able to identify this identity without someone having to take on the disheveled defeated defective head-bent-down shuffle of ashamed victim? Can you walk with your head held high and shoulders back and still be read as a survivor?

Can you wear a dress and still be read as a dyke?

The answer to both of these questions, I think, is No.

Victims of sexual abuse learn to pass as *something*—perfectionists, inherently damaged persons, or both. Both draw the attention away from the abuse. Like leeching.

You can't see what this is that's hiding me. It's a weird shroud coloring my vision but not yours. I learn to pass as a human being, as not-a-molester, as not-a-rapist.

How can I claim for myself what is lost? How can I be alone in this cadence? Outside it is crisp, clean, lonely blue-gray night turning into morning, turning the regressive forgetting, aggressive outstanding faces of night, surely sleeting.

The survivor has nothing but her body to put between herself and the captor/rapist. My body passes between us while I escape elsewhere (sometimes) during the assaults themselves. My body is the only thing of danger, and the only thing I have to wield. I learn to pass it elsewhere, learn to pass it between myself and others, learn to control its passing, its deliberation and consideration.

The armor is like safety. The armor is like rock and we have no walls to hide behind. We become the armor. We become the rock. We pass ourselves as we would have you take us. We create ourselves in our own image and decry liberalism and defy licentiousness and take on ourselves as our own best enemy and call ourselves something like whole and declare our own names true. And some of us are still hiding. To be rid of him and acceptable to you, to the sense of you that we have integrated in ourselves.

Lots of femmes describe "the nod"—the look, the smile of recognition—that acknowledgment they don't receive. The "What are you doing here?" look that they get in its place. Just recently, another self-identified butch says, *Hey, if I see you in the video store, and you look feminine to me, I'm gonna assume that you're straight.* Meaning, of course, I'm going to exclude you from my community. And this from someone who supposedly has some understanding of butch and femme, the history, the reality and the *existence* of femme dykes.

It takes *work* to continue to ignore the fact that some self-identified dykes/lesbians/queer women are not masculine-acting/appearing or in some surface appearance/visual way, gender-non-normative. We are many of us gender non-normative behaviorally, and when those actions/behaviors are noticed and taken into account, we might be given the benefit of some doubt (or maybe just taken for a "right-on straight girl"?). But it's surface I'm talking about, the embodied body and the tactics of exclusion, of defining community with a glance, calling you in or out.

I often come to the decision to exclude butches and other masculine-gendered dykes/lesbians/queers from my gaze. I will not allow them acceptability into *my* community. Granted, my little individual protest doesn't matter when my eyes aren't attended to in the first place (and, you know, my protest comes to a quick end when I choose to acknowledge my butch lover). Still, it gives me a little stab of pleasure to willfully not-see these demanding revelations of recognized/recognizable queerness. It's true that, for a split second, I want every butch I see silently dripping desire only momentarily because, outside of that quiet vault, I don't want to give them the power of my satisfaction, the visual cues of my desire, while they're ignoring me with such precision. I watch them, though, when I think they're not looking, like they're a silent salient separate species, like they don't belong to me: they've become some remote tribe or they always were. And when I say I wouldn't give them the satisfaction, I mean that I don't want to give them any more power over me: the power of recognition, of surety, the power of the masculine over the feminine.

But move away from my lust and get back to the tactics of exclusion and inclusion: to ignore, to consciously and willfully avoid acknowledgment—is that also a survival skill, internalized by those who are more consistently noticed and attended to by society at large, demonized, hated; a desire to protect, as well as internalized self-hate? *She can't be like (as bad as) me; look at her.* Or is it self-protective, like: *The last time I hit on a woman I wasn't 100 percent certain was queer, or who didn't look gay like me, I got the shit kicked out of me by (insert your choice of misogynist male "protectors" here).* Or is it the (identity) politics of similarity: *We're just like everybody else, and if you want a piece of this pie, you better be like me.* Is it really just an internalization of the wholesale '70s rejection of all things apparently and ostensibly patriarchal, the gender-neutral (read: butch) rejection of femininity that the whole community was supposed to conform to—notice how the masculine leads the charge again? And didn't I do it too? Who is to blame here when we flow through the gendered this way?

I'm trying to figure out the root cause of this active denial on the part of so many in my dyke "community"(-ies) who deny/ignore the existence of femmes, of other dykes who (seem to) look like everything that various foremothers fought against. And me, as well. Didn't I ignore and even despise femmes? How can I come up now with an *I* and a *we* and an *us* and a *them* and put myself on the side of the girls? I'm lost here, in my indignation and fear.

It's one thing to have a man (straight? apparently—he passes as straight, to me) assume that I am straight. It's a different enactment of power (over? under?) for a visibly-read dyke to assume that I am not gay.

In becoming a boy, I had a desire to be seen in all the ways my stepfather would hate, as everything he would oppose: un-femininity, un-selection of men. I espoused everything I thought my mother should have, in her claim to feminism. I wanted to be everyone's stereotype lesbian. When I described myself as looking like *an average dyke, just like every other lesbian in town*, it was a thoughtless statement, betraying my willful blindness to femme dykedom (and all the other dykenesses that don't look like the currently popular close-cropped-boi thing) and revealed a desire to become that which I described myself as.

It was a mistake, and it wasn't. I enjoyed the visibility, calculated and treacherous. Queerness was, for me, the opposite of my survivorhood, which no one could see, because as a part of surviving itself, I had to learn how to pass as unproblematic.

I created my dykeness as a problem, wore it like a skin, made it visible. Masculine or butch dykeness was a salve, something put on, protective and predatory. I was turning the tables.

We're not supposed to do that, and if we do, we're not supposed to say it. Party line in femme-butch community is the (still, continued) sense and representation of an innate gender, something we've always known about ourselves (even if we didn't have the words for it) and always held true to, never betrayed. Betrayal. I am that betrayer. I talk about when I was a boy, and how I've shifted. I lay claim to both/and.

I kept a copy of Joan Nestle's *The Persistent Desire: A Femme-Butch Reader* on my bookshelf for seven or eight years before I read the femme parts. I found them offensive, suspect, inconsequential, weak, catty, whiny. Damning stereotypes that could be applied only to me, the too-vehement displacement of my own internal judgment. And now, I am unlearning all that I trained myself into with respect to dykeness (that, yes, began with straight stereotyping, the stepfather's hostility toward dykes, my own desire to become what it was I was attracted to, having conflated those, unable to separate my own power as distinct and unique from that which I desired).

Does it make sense to be angry with "my" community because I don't pass in *my own eyes*?

It occurred to me last night that I just feel resigned about my gender, resigned to my sexuality, like I'm tired of fighting (for) something I can't have. I'm petulant and scared but mostly off-the-side resigned, out in the way-back machine, deep shuffling into the fact that I didn't win: I am a girl, and I am seen and hidden as a girl, off to the inside, far in the guts of gender. I no longer "work" as queer, and I am tired of trying and being disappointed. The everyday reach for eye contact, for *Hello*, for recognition, like it's somebody else's business to accept me into my own tribe. These are my tired eyes. Leave me the cues and I'll use them, but I'm wrecked on my own shores.

It's like that old saying: you can't please anybody, so you might as well be alone. (Actually, I don't think that's the saying. I think it's: you can't please everybody, so you might as well just please yourself. Whatever. They're both exhausting.)

I am so tired of disappearing after I say, *This is how I am and feel,* and those others reply, *No, we don't think you really fit.* How do I unlearn that undeliverance?

She passes the test. But whose? We're jaded, shaded, judged every day by everyone else's eyes, given pass or fail, a glance over, an examination. What I feel now, think, sense, and have had shown to me is that I pass as a straight white girl with long hair and a thinnish and roundish body, with paint on my fingers toes eyes lips. What do I base this on? The fact that men are the only ones who will make eye contact with me? The fact that I look more now like women I see in the magazines or on TV (or around me everywhere) than I did when I was a boy? The fact that my attempts to flirt with or be recognized by women I read as gay are often passed by? Maybe these women aren't gay. It's my own conflation of masculine with womanhood that makes dyke in my eyes, anyway; I'm still unlearning that myself. What I see are the boidykes, the butches, the ones I was (trying to be): the flamboyant excursion into queerness.

It's true that I appreciate, viscerally, how my lover passes (as butch *and* as male, thereby already accepted into the community I longed for), and at the same time, sie constantly battles through society's antagonism in response to hir gender-ambiguity, the blurring confusion that sharpens to anger through fear when someone has assumed hir male and then reads hir as female. As black male, that is, and then as black female, that is: and all the threats to hir safety that slam up on one side of that wall and fall down on top of hir on the other.

We two face physical threats emanating from the same beam of power, that solid rise of sexism and racism. They are not the same threats. They are the flip sides of one another.

I question myself regularly in my need for that deviation from whatever a norm could mean. It's true that I am outside of things and my lover, sie is more so, and so we are more familiar with the fringes, with looking through for the blades of grass in a current of sludge.

A single experience of visibility and un-invisibleness breaks the ice and anger of me. Someone, a stranger to me, reads and approaches me, assuming queerness. But is it my burgeoning comfort with myself that allows for the connection?

I've recently gone through a mourning period for my passing-dyke-hood and have come out on the other side of resistance, to resignation. I don't pass (and I do). I want to stop trying to make friendly communal eye contact, that establishment of casual community, the thing that extends home into body, onto the bus, onto the street, or the straight bar or the doctor's office or the mall. The look that says, *Sure, you're safe here.* Not that I'd know that would ever be true. But as a survivor, for this survivor, I was looking for safety and home. I wanted the strangers who would first read me and then protect me, wanted "family" that meant more than devastation.

Thus the mourning period. I'm unmarked now and, as before, as when I was a high school student being regularly raped and held psychologically captive (but read at school as only a slut or excessive or eccentric, but not "troubled,"—it was the white skin and class privilege that got in my way there), I am unseen. I pass away. I pass into the nothingness of white, middle-class straight normality, of invisibility.

Once again, I decide I will defy my own training and offer my looks and smiles only at the apparently-feminine-gendered beings I see around—we will pass into each other through our own swollen eyes. But they are swollen shut. Feminine-gendered beings don't look at one another; we have been taught that we must look to the masculine-gendered beings for approval. We look to make sure we pass with them. And, okay, it's a safety issue—not passing (which way?) can mean violence: you must be the right balance of gender and body. Too much feminine is dangerous, even on an XX body, but particularly if the body is XY.

There is nothing cautious or delicate about the fact that I pass as a straight woman. It's the default setting, brute force algorithm: yes or no. Check it against the model, and if it looks all right, throw it in that bin over there. I pulled out of it for a while, but I have fallen back.

I am resigned to being read as more normal than I really am. I learned that passing lesson during the mornings I came to school still sticky with my stepfather all over me, the days I knew I'd have to go back home to more of the same. Not allowing my terror to be read was a survival skill, a lifesaving necessity: it's true. And, for Christ's sake, I passed to the *mother*—why shouldn't I pass to the guidance counselors and teachers? I thought I was that good. I thought I could do it again and again, re-incarnate again and again.
   But I got tired. And lonely.

Hir black passing butch and my white femme: we make quite a calculated couple. Newly visible, but what do they see, and how much does that matter? Our passings are entirely different. We walk through two completely different consignments of our bodies, the public designation of myself and yourself. How sie is seen as vagrant and threat and I am seen as property and waste.

I have been fighting for many years against (becoming) how I am seen now. When do we know what we are is not how we see(m)? When did I know I was being seen as my stepfather crafted?

I get so tired of trying to explain what I'm talking about. I say the same things over and over and I don't care anymore in this bedroom, in this office, on this bench. Did the door to my deep desire click open when I was seen, clocked as both gay and feminine, or did it click when I set myself free with hir, or when I just knew why I was doing so? I *am* this gay queer entity, even if sie is a man, even if I am pressed in skirts. It's not a straight thing, and it doesn't matter if it is. I've grown tired of wanting to be masked. I don't know if you will see me and I don't know if I will care anymore. You never see me; I never see you. Behind your surfaces are all of your multiplicities. It takes time to be there.

Sex and the Single Septuagenarian
Liz Langley

A few years ago there was a popular Pepsi commercial featuring presidential candidate and Viagra spokesman Bob Dole watching Britney Spears dance on TV. At the end of the ad, a dog sitting at Dole's side barks at the set. "Easy, boy," says Dole to the pooch—though I always thought it was slyly implied that he was actually talking to his own reanimated wiener.

This three-alarm image of the senator erect is uncomfortable on a lot of levels, but the most obvious is that people aren't used to thinking of seniors in a sexual way and aren't in a rush to start. We love to see Grandma and Grandpa running marathons, volunteering, and taking tap class. But imagining them doing the mattress mambo is another story.

Senior sexuality is certainly important in Florida, the oldest state in the country, and where, according to the U.S. Census Bureau, 17 percent of the population was sixty-five or over as of July

1, 2005. And those seniors aren't just sitting home playing bridge: In "Sexuality at Midlife and Beyond," a 2004 update to a 1999 AARP survey, more than half of respondents, aged forty-five and up, cited sexual activity as a critical part of good relationships and as an important factor in quality of life. Eighty-four percent disagreed or strongly disagreed that "sex is only for young people" and reported having intimate experiences once a week, ranging from kissing to intercourse. In September of 2006, the CNBC Special Report "Boomer Nation" reported that over-fifty singles make up Match.com's fastest-growing demographic. "People are orgasmic well into their nineties," says Sallie Foley, director for the Center for Sexual Health at the University of Michigan Health System, author, and "Modern Love" columnist for the AARP magazine. A sex therapist, Foley recently had a client who experienced her first orgasm at sixty-seven.

Of course, lives—and libidos—don't end at fifty. But a growing concern is that the same parents and grandparents who once scolded their kids for playing outside without coats may not always be covering up where it counts beneath the sheets. According to Tom Liberti, chief of the Bureau of HIV/AIDS for the Florida Department of Health, 16 percent of newly reported HIV cases in 2005 were in people over fifty. Numbers on other sexually transmitted diseases don't suggest that they're spreading like wildfire among seniors (though not all STDs are necessarily reported to the DOH). Still, with more older singles than ever, well, you know the sex talk your parents dreaded having with you when you were a kid? Now you might want to have a similar one with them. (Well, *want* might be taking it a bit far.)

Viagra and other erectile dysfunction drugs have enabled seniors to have active sex lives longer into their golden years, but those same seniors are typically not targeted with information about safety. "People don't want to think about it," says Jim Campbell, president of the National Association on HIV Over Fifty. It's an attitude he likens to "Everyone else's kid is having sex except mine." Campbell's group recently helped one nursing home establish a room for conjugal visits that couples can reserve like a hotel room. He doesn't want to say which nursing home, though, because talk of sexual matters tends to cause such consternation.

"One of our counselors has a one-hundred-year-old man with HIV," says Jolene Mullins, an early intervention consultant with the Broward County Health Department's Senior HIV Intervention Project. "He's newly diagnosed and how he got it we'll probably never know," though she does say sexual contact is the prime transmission method of the virus in the older population, along with some needle sharing. But consider: even if he had been infected twenty-five years ago, it still would have been at age seventy-five.

Hang on to that thought and now remember how resistant older people can be to new things. I once asked my own mother why she didn't use the microwave and she said, defiantly, "Because I'm too old." If seniors are slow to adapt to cell phones, how about using condoms? In their day they were strictly for birth control—perhaps the one health concern that seniors, luxuriously, don't have to worry about.

"I never heard the word 'condom' till I don't know when. We whispered the word 'rubber,'" says Jane Fowler, seventy-one. Even now, she jokingly rushes over the word in a phone interview from her Kansas City home. Jane has a sparkling laugh and the sweetest, most Marion Cunningham voice I've ever heard. She was diagnosed with HIV at the age of fifty-five and eventually cofounded the National Association on HIV Over Fifty, is cofounder and director of HIV Wisdom for Older Women, and works as an HIV/AIDS educator, speaking to groups all across the country.

In 1991 Fowler got a letter from an insurance company she'd applied to for coverage and was shocked to find she had been denied. "My blood had disclosed a significant abnormality," she says, though the letter didn't say what it was. She remembered someone had come by and stuck her finger. "He left with my application and my deposit and my blood and I didn't think any more about it, especially the blood, until I got this letter."

Using datebook diaries that go back to 1958, Fowler was able to trace not just the approximate time she was infected, but the day. After twenty-three years of marriage, she had unwillingly been divorced, and after a while she started dating. "I had a few intimacies," she said. "[I wasn't] out there sleeping around…I didn't fit the stereotype," Fowler explains, and so wasn't the kind of person anyone would figure to test. The man she was seeing when she was infected was someone she had known for a long time. "He is not alive today," she says.

It makes Fowler cringe when she hears about seniors who practice what she sees as a kind of willful naïveté. She picks a few names "out of the thirties" to illustrate her point. "So, you've got Betty and she's announced that she started dating Jack and she's so comfortable because she's known him for so long. She knew Jack when he was married to Mary. Then Mary died. Betty does not know what Jack was doing or what Mary was doing. You don't know what's going on in somebody's bedroom, or outside of it. I found that out myself."

People tell her, "I'm so thankful that I'm with Herb because I just never have anything to worry about." Fowler laughs. "And you think, 'Okay, Marge, okay.'" Still, she says, "It's hard to stand up in front of women and suggest to them that their partner, significant other, whatever, might be having experiences outside this primary relationship."

Jolene Mullins, of the Broward County Health Department, says another concern is senior men who are gay or bisexual and may not have been able to be open about their sexuality in the past—and might not think of HIV as affecting their generation. "I can't tell you how many seniors say, 'This is not my problem,' " Mullins says. "[They ask], 'Why are you even talking to us?' "

A big part of that attitude relates to America's timidity in talking about sex, in Fowler's opinion. Older people are especially reluctant to do so—and often their health-care providers don't ask. Doctors see someone who looks like their grandmother and think, "I'm not going to ask this person about sex!"

Tom Liberti, of the Florida Department of Health, says he's spoken to med students at Florida State University's School of Medicine about that very issue. "If a sixty- or seventy-year-old presents at a doctor's office with medical symptoms like losing weight…the doctor isn't necessarily going to think of HIV," but the virus doesn't discriminate. Jane Fowler offers doctors another way of looking at it: "An older person, in the confines of a provider's office, might even enjoy bragging a little bit."

Though methods of diagnosis (like the thirty-minute HIV test) and medication have improved considerably, testing can still be a scary experience for anyone—but especially for seniors who are uncomfortable discussing their intimate secrets. Fortunately, Miriam Schuler, an eighty-seven-year-old Fort Lauderdale widow, is the adorable embodiment of the Sue Johanson/Dr. Ruth effect (the one that makes frank sexual messages seem easier to hear from older women). "I've been called 'the Condom Grandma,' " Schuler says, for her volunteer work handing out condoms on behalf of Broward County's Senior HIV Intervention Project, mostly at health fairs. She even gives me a handful, a sign she is clearly more optimistic about my love life than I am.

Schuler tells me she shows passersby a picture of a dress made out of condoms and asks, "Do you think I should wear this to my granddaughter's wedding?" Sometimes senior men will tell her, "I'm too old for this," and she'll give them a condom anyway and say, "Put it in your pocket. Make your friends jealous." She encourages grandparents to send condoms to their grandkids with the birthday check and a note that says, "We love you. Be safe."

Tom Liberti says that when the numbers of HIV-infected seniors in Florida climbed up to 11 percent, the Department of Health started looking at ways to reach seniors, like putting more mature faces on their health posters. Schuler is a perfect example of what an asset older people can be to their own community, simply by communicating the idea that condoms aren't just for birth control anymore.

"I can tell you the attitude of the men," says one sixty-six-year-old woman I speak to on the phone. They come from an era where they didn't use protection, and "they think, 'I'll be dead from old age before I die of AIDS.' " She protects her friends' identities and doesn't want hers used, but says some singles insist on sexual safety, and even knows one couple who broke up over the idea. "She said she wouldn't have sex without protection. He said he wouldn't have sex with protection. That was the end of that."

A few days later, I'm tooling down the Florida Turnpike for an evening out at the Villages, a retirement community so large it covers part of three counties in central Florida. Dozens of golf carts are parked outside the shops and restaurants of the Spanish Springs Town Square like a parody of the motorcycles that line the streets during Bike Week in Daytona. My companions and I have been invited to Katie Belle's Resident Club, for Villagers only, and the vastness of the two-story nightspot and the din inside come as a surprise. The saloon-style interior is heavy on carved wood and stained glass, as if you dropped a disco into a Bob Evans, only more posh. Our hostess is a well-dressed bundle of energy, and her generosity in introducing friends—and theirs in chatting—makes it a disarmingly warm and welcoming place.

The crowds are so dense that people stand on the staircase, their ages ranging from collegiate to septuagenarian, though heavy on the latter. I get ankle-deep into the merlot with a number of residents, a band called Rocky and the Rollers plays classics, and the emcee announces that Katie Belle's will be open all the way until 11:00 p.m. Turns out there are other clubs people typically move on to when they're looking for a late night. I ask a woman sitting beside me if she does much dating.

"What?"

"Dating."

"What?"

"Dating."

"Dancing?"

"DATING!"

To be fair, it's loud in there.

She's single, loves life in the Villages, but needn't date as she has "a steady" whom she calls "my fiancé." When I ask when the wedding is she looks at me like I'm bananas. "I was married for thirty years and engaged for fifteen," she says. At her age she evidently has no interest in making another such commitment.

Another woman, trim and prim, isn't nuts about the dating scene, partly because there's just too much competition. Everyone I talk with consistently cites female-male ratios of around eight-to-one, making the men sound like kids in a candy store.

One Village guy tells me that he's "very concerned" about STDs, but doesn't use protection all that much. I ask one of the women if her friends worry about protection.

"Yes," she says, "but they don't follow through" on their concerns.

"How do you know?" I ask.

"Because I didn't. I said I would, and I didn't."

After hitting three clubs, throwing back quite a few, hearing karaoke—not to mention a lot of thoughts about love, life, and lingerie—and dancing with a charming seventy-five-year-old man, I conclude that my new septuagenarian friends and I have more in common than I imagined. I remember how, days earlier, one of my sources had asked me my age.

"I'm forty-one," I answered.

"Whatever is going on with you at forty-one," she said, "is going on with us."

This is not to single out the Villages as a den of vice; it had enough trouble after a story concerning the rapid rise of STDs there appeared on the local news—a report some residents rolled their eyes at as "overblown." Jolene Mullins says that the socialization in a place like the Villages might mean there are more sexual opportunities, but doesn't discount that seniors who live in regular neighborhoods and congregate at community centers also find sexual partners. Still, she says "the reality is that in those communities you've got seven females for every male."

Former Villages public relations director Bob Mervine has his own take. By and large, these are people "who grew up at a time when sex, drugs, and rock 'n' roll were forbidden," he explains. "Now those things are normal, everyday parts of their lives. They think they are in heaven. All the booze, all the sex in the world, and all the time to enjoy them."

Two weeks later, in Broward County, I find myself in a very different kind of senior center, a single building, whose literature describes it as "an independent senior living community." Instead of a lavish town square, I enter the subdued building, hushed and pleasant. I've arrived on a weekday afternoon for an HIV screening, which is a lot different than happy hour. It's not quite unhappy hour either, though. There is ice cream.

Edid Gonzáles, outreach coordinator for Broward County's SHIP program, says most of the seniors she tries to educate and offers to test for HIV think she's giving them good information to pass on to their grandchildren. They don't get right away that it's for them.

Nine people file in and out of a community room while Gonzáles, bearing a bag full of black condoms (well, it's almost Halloween) the size of a throw pillow, is here. No one thinks he or she needs the information, but almost everyone is attentive, supportive, talkative, and curious. They all ask questions, like why there is no vaccination program for HIV and whether the virus can be spread through saliva. Calvin Sprague, sixty-six, tells Edid, "I'm one-hundred percent behind what you're doing." One woman mentions that she saw a commercial that said the effect of "that pill" can last up to four hours. "In four hours," she says, "you could screw the whole building."

No one gets tested.

Gentle, soft-spoken Gonzáles tries to make one of these presentations every day in hopes of reaching more South Florida seniors. For those who believe "something else will kill me first," Gonzáles' colleague Jolene Mullins says, "The virus attacks the immune system and your immune system naturally breaks down with aging. If HIV is put on top of that, it naturally enhances the problems." Then there is the challenge of seniors who have other serious illnesses, like diabetes, and must battle HIV on top of them. The complex interaction of medications is just one more risk for doctors to consider.

It all comes down to prevention. Jane Fowler has a special maxim she likes to use at her presentations that brings it all back to Bob Dole. Back when Dole was doing ads that said it took courage to talk to your doctor about erectile dysfunction, Fowler thought he should have advocated safety, too. She even offered a line: "Now, if you can get it up, cover it up."

The Pink Ghetto (A Four-Part Series)
Lux Nightmare
and Melissa Gira

Lux Nightmare: Welcome to NSFW

At one of my offices (I have several), I cannot access Sexerati.

If I attempt to go to this site, I am presented with a spare white page that informs me that this site has been blocked for being "Adult/Sexually Explicit."

The same filtering software blocks me from viewing a bunch of sex education sites: a vaguely inconvenient/ironic situation, given that I work as a sex educator.

When you work in sex—as a sex blogger, a sex educator, a pornographer, whatever—and you're trying to promote both yourself and your work, you are pretty much guaranteed to come up against some very hard walls.

Ask your friends to subscribe to your RSS feed: they can't have the word *sex* on their work computer. Ask your blogger friends to promote your project: they can't, it'd fuck with the vibe they're going for. Try to get advertisers, try to promote your work, try to sell things using Paypal:

You have now entered the Pink Ghetto.

I've been using the Internet to talk about sex, in one form or another, since I was eighteen: basically, since it was legal to do so. Most of my work online has been firmly confined in the Pink Ghetto: it's the kind of stuff I can't show to certain types of people, the kind of stuff that people erase from their browser history.

Even when it's not porn, it's sex: and sex alone is enough to earn the label NSFW—Not Safe for Work. Sex, even academic sex, is something we can't always discuss in polite company. Trying to build your life, your career, around a discussion of sex means accepting that you will always have a fringe identity. That no matter how academic, how smart, how clean you keep it, you will always be on the edges of polite society. You will always be in the Pink Ghetto, and you will never be able to escape it.

Melissa Gira: Nowhere to Go But Slut

When thinking sex online, porn operates as the great dividing line. As those who work sex online, that's the frame we're issued—are you porn, or not porn? Explicit, or nonexplicit? Adult, or "family friendly"? Safe for work, or...? *Whose* work, really? What if writing, blogging, and thinking sex *is* your work?

Porn—making it, reviewing it, theorizing in best sellers about it—is only just one way to make a living thinking sex, yet porn is still the culture's point of reference for sex. This framing of sex online as being either *porn* or *not-porn* doesn't just come to us by way of the culture alone. Rather, it is enforced by the structure of our publishing and media industries, which themselves are, in turn, shaped by the culture's attitudes toward sex. Anyone contributing to the sex culture by reflecting on, educating about, or otherwise talking sex is subject to answering for their work's ability to arouse—and if it does arouse, how much can it still educate? Being smart about sex and being a sexual smarty-pants are still viewed as mutually exclusive positions, whether we're talking sex academia, sex in publishing, or the sex entertainment industry.

What to do for those of us contributing to the sex culture with our words and pictures, no matter how naked we are or aren't in them? Do we limit our work to abstraction and theory, talking only in the vague and general "you" of the culture as a way not only to seem more credible, but to shield ourselves from being viewed as sluts? Who would care about these things, after all, but sluts? Who would want to make a living from engaging the culture at large around sexuality? What kind of person can know so much about human sexuality and can still put a sentence together about it? Just as some people harbor suspicions about "the sex people" as their own form of defense and distancing, so that they don't have to deal with the possibility of sex being just part of *being*, so, too, are we "sex people" asked to make apologies for our work if we want to "be accepted."

So, in this context, I could say I'm only doing this—this sex thing on the Internet—to get somewhere else in my career, as a stepping stone to some supposedly elevated ground as a real writer, a real journalist, a real contributor to society. Sex is a commodity, that's for sure, but it's only really socially acceptable to traffic in temporarily. Where once upon a time, the story of sex for women was from virgin to whore, in the story of the business of sex writing, there's the chance for all us soiled doves to reclaim our purity by renouncing sex, relegating sex to "that crazy thing" we wrote about to get our start, revising not just our resumes but our passions.

What if sex is where you want to go, not just your rent as you get there? (Hey, it's been my rent, too, not knocking that for a millisecond.) What if sex is your work, not limited to prostitution or porn or what we think of as sex work, but as your medium? What is so less noble about thinking sex rather than money, rather than politics, religion, or art? Sex being so fully embedded in the human experience, I want to put out there that there really is no way to engage the culture on "what *really* matters" without looking at sexuality.

Producing sexual media, theorizing, studying, and educating about sex are not some marginal activity, or at least, they should be thought of as such no longer. For those of us working sex, refusing to be ghettoized for our labors and loves doesn't mean "rising up" from the gutter, but resisting the idea that sex is in some gutter *at all*.

Lux Nightmare: Where Everyone Knows (and Doesn't Know) Your Name

When you're trying to promote yourself—both online and off—it helps to develop a recognizable brand. As the Internet has grown, developed, and professionalized, it's become common to see people making use of it to build a brand identity, and even more common for that brand to be one's real name.

I've always been interested in using the Internet as a tool for building a brand: back when I ran a porn site I created accounts on every social networking site I could find, using the profiles to raise my visibility and promote my projects. I've done a great deal to put my name out there, to make my name synonymous with sex education, with smart dialogue about sex, with quality erotica. And I've done a pretty good job: in a lot of circles, Lux Nightmare creates an immediate association with all the things I want to stand for.

There's just one catch.

My name isn't really my name.

This is the problem of making a career in sex: as much as you want to promote yourself, put your name out there, become a recognizable figure; as much as you want everyone to know your name; there's a certain fear that one day you'll need to go "legit," that one day having your real name easily associated with smut won't be the best career move.

This is, again, the problem with doing work that lives in the Pink Ghetto.

I'm not ashamed of the work I do, or the work I've done. I'm not ashamed to have my image or voice or brand associated with smart work around sex. And I want to say that it's just a short step away from associating this work with my real name.

But I'm a realist, and I know that putting my real name on work that's just a hop, skip, and a jump from porn means getting myself blackballed (pinkballed?) from any kind of "legitimate" work. Doing porn under a pseudonym is not an act of shame, it's an act of self-protection. Being out as someone who has worked in porn, someone who works on the fringe of sex advocacy and education, would ultimately jeopardize my safety, my sanity—not to mention the sex education work that I do out in the real world, under my real name.

It should be noted, of course, that there are people who do work around sex and *do* use their real names (Rachel Kramer Bussel, Tristan Taormino, and Jamye Waxman immediately spring to mind). But these people are often the exception to the rule and perhaps, most tellingly, these are often people who started their work as writers, edging into the Pink Ghetto after a professional reputation had already been established.

A few months ago, I was interviewed by Wendy Shalit about my involvement in porn. I told her that I had left the industry, moved on, largely because I couldn't handle the weight of stigmatized work; couldn't handle the ghettoized nature of what I was doing. And it's true, and to a degree it still holds.

I would love to put my real name out there, to unite my "legitimate" work with my stigmatized work and tell the world that I'm proud of it all, that it's all an important part of my fight for sexual literacy, for sexual knowledge and freedom and education. I would love to take a stand like that. But I can't. There is too much to lose, too much at stake, and for now, it's not a battle I'm prepared to fight.

With Stigma Comes Opportunity

It would be very easy to write piece after piece complaining about the frustration of working from a stigmatized place, to rail against the system that tells us that sex is dirty, that interest in sex is necessarily prurient, that we must hide any and all discussions of sex behind a filter of NSFW.

It would be very easy to do that; it would also be very depressing and relatively pointless. And so, in the fourth installment of the Pink Ghetto, I would like to take a moment to reflect on some of the more positive aspects of operating out of stigmatized territory.

When I was twenty years old, I was a CEO. I was getting interviewed for pieces in respectable national publications, I was being treated as an authority in my chosen field. People respected what I had to say, and even today, even after several years of keeping a low profile, I still get requests for interviews. My opinion, thoughts, and experiences are still valued, still treated as worthwhile.

I got that, I got to this place, because I wasn't afraid of stepping into the Pink Ghetto; even more so, because I was willing to bring my best efforts, to bring talent and care and charisma, to my Pink Ghetto work. I didn't shy away from the stigma: I gave it my all.

And because I was one of relatively few people willing to do that, I stood out. I gained notoriety. I gained a voice.

I hate the stigma that comes with the work that I do. I'm also fully aware that it is the stigma that makes it so appealing. I go to the places that I go because the aura of the Pink Ghetto frightens away other talented individuals, and in doing so, in being willing to take the risks that I take, I stake out this land as my world, my area of expertise.

I would love to live in a world where the study of sexuality is viewed on the same level as any other academic discipline, where a healthy attitude toward sexuality is recognized as a fundamental part of a healthy lifestyle. I don't live in that world, not yet, and so I am happy, eager, to fight for that world, even if it means slipping into the Pink Ghetto. Even if it means taking on the weight, the oppression, the fear of the stigma in order to do it. With stigma comes opportunity, and embracing the stigma of the Pink Ghetto, taking it head-on, has given me opportunities and experiences far beyond any I might have achieved out in the mainstream world.

To Have or Have Not: Sex on the Wedding Night
Jill Eisenstadt

Four a.m, one hour till dawn, and our four-star suite was still full
of revelers. One hour in which to get out of our wedding clothes,
tally the gift checks, have sex.

It was our wedding night. Of course we'd do it. This I truly believed despite the hour. Blame it on bridal magazines, Hollywood
or my own naïveté, but when I agreed to take part in the marriage rites I assumed that meant all of them. Why else would I have
worn the (new) white gown, the (old) tiara and the (borrowed)
garter that gave me prickly heat? Why would I have held up the
ceremony to shove something blue (a Canada Dry label) into my
cleavage? Why would I have let my father "give me away?" Maybe
it was unrealistic to expect an all-night bubble bath erotica. But
surely our vows would be consummated. For all I knew, our license
wasn't even valid otherwise: unravished come sunrise, I'd turn into
a pumpkin, or worse—a single girl again.

That I hadn't technically been a girl in a while only heightened my anticipation. What could be more intense than a second chance to lose your innocence? This time without pain or hair-trigger conclusion. What more fitting way to mark the commitment to exclusive lovemaking till death (or divorce) did us part than with "le petit mort," as the French like to call orgasm, preferably followed by rebirth and fireworks. After years of "sin," what could be more thrilling than the inaugural bedding of a legally married woman?

Unfortunately, I had to wait for the answers to these questions. It appears that a great many us have had to wait. "Did you or didn't you?" I began asking friends and acquaintances over the months, then years that followed my wedding. Not the most scientific method, yet the response were revealing. Many laughed nervously, evaded the question, changed the subject. But the overwhelming majority finally gave an excuse:

"Bladder infection. I cried."

"Mono. I was contagious."

"Spent the whole night on a plane."

"…in a car."

"…sitting in traffic."

"…stuck at the airport."

"…mile after mile of no vacancy signs."

"We fought about what he said to my high school friends."

"…fought with that cheapskate caterer."

"…fought about my ex-husband."

"Pillow fight."

"Morning sickness… Yes, at night."

Of the few who did claim victory, only one ever described the act as being anything out of the ordinary. And I quote: "…A little like date rape." The others just thought they "had to" or "should." They just "did it" to "do it." Laugh we might, but somehow, we still feel we're just supposed to have sex on our wedding nights. When we don't we think of it as a bad omen. Or as one friend, Tara, put it: "I felt like we'd flunked some kind of test."

After years of living together, she and her fiancé Bill had spent a chaste prenuptial week in separate (but equal) apartments. He wasn't allowed a preview of her "virginal" gown. She wasn't allowed a review of his "worldly" bachelor party. From the proposal on bended knee to the send-off under a shower of politically incorrect white rice, they'd performed their traditional bride and groom roles flawlessly.

"We had the honeymoon suite with a king-size water bed, the complimentary champagne, the works...." But then something—or rather nothing—happened. "We conked out."

"Blacked out."

"Crashed. The whole wedding party in a big pile."

Barring the religious, most people nowadays wouldn't dream of marrying somebody with whom they hadn't slept. Common sense says that ignorance is dangerous. Better to know the body to which you're pledging monogamy. Rule out incompatible fetishes and irreparable conditions. Decide you like the bed you're getting into. A lot. Marrying later, we're hardly naïve. So what's all this hullabaloo over a one-shot screw? Why is everyone still playing the same old game, pretending that the bride is still a virgin?

In earlier times, that kind of false advertising would have gotten a girl stoned to death. Those bloody sheets had to be hung out as proof. If the marriage was deemed void, she might be sent into a life of prostitution or perhaps, worse, back to her father's house, shamed.

If nothing else, the number of sexually experienced brides today makes punishing all of them impractical. It was with the invention of latex and dependable condoms that women in the Western world began taking the risk. Reports from 1920 show only 50 percent of brides in this country at that time were virgins. The difference was they didn't sleep with the men they were marrying. Tricky chicks, eh? Makes you wonder over their wedding night scenarios. Maybe they fooled their new husbands too. Maybe they learned to fake not having an orgasm. But more likely they were just like us.

"Too exhausted," for intercourse. Planning a wedding is said to rate in the top five for stress, along with air-traffic controlling and death of a spouse.

"Too hungry." Only those who elope get to eat at their weddings. And brides typically don't eat for weeks before either.

"Too preoccupied." Partying.

"Too drunk." If too preoccupied.

"Too hungover." If the wedding was over before nightfall.

"Too many buttons. Forty or more buttons. I swear, I gave up."

"He couldn't get it up. All of a sudden."

I heard all these reasons and most of them thrice. But all I really heard was that no one is having sex on their wedding nights anymore. It's the best kept undirty secret around. So why is it secret? It's not rational. It's ritual. And when you examine it (which is exactly what is not done with rituals), the whole subtext of the celebration is sex. Once that veil goes up and you may now kiss the bride, you must keep kissing her whenever a spoon hits crystal. You must dance the first dance to your song. You must cut the first slice of cake and take turns smooshing it into each other's waiting mouths. There's the high jinx with the garter and the getaway in the vandalized, shoe-festooned vehicle.

It's a performance—flirting for an audience. It's pretense and foreplay. It's one outdated formality after another, leading to the ultimate climax—sex. Even my ride over the threshold (a vestige of marriage-by-capture) had cheerleaders, though their presence ruled out the very act for which they rooted. Regardless of what the customs or trappings suggested, I'm sure not a single one of them believed I was a virgin. And why should anyone, most of all myself, care? Marriage is a public declaration of love. Sex is a private declaration of marriage. Or should be.

But if we no longer measure a bride's worth by her chastity, then why do we continue to behave as if we do? Why suffer old men who wink and tell the groom they hope he gets "lucky?" Why sit through the never-ending tasteless jokes and tactless toasts or worry, as I did, over scary old wives tales, i.e., "The first in bed will be the first to die."

Maybe the place to start would be an update of that all-important mother-daughter "chat." Brides-to-be still need to know the score. So tell her marriage requires work and compromise, humor and friendship, trust and lust. And if you don't manage to have sex on your wedding night, rest assured. Someone else will. Weddings are, after all, notoriously romantic for the guests.

Take the pressure off and fresh customs would have room to evolve. Modern newlyweds might start to, say, share a banana split, exchange foot massages…Talk.

But when I found myself fully dressed the next morning, I wasn't thinking so clearly. Was the marriage off to a bad start? I fretted. Would our plane crash, our passions wane, our eyes wander? Were we doomed to a future of peck-like kisses?

Fluorescent light dinners? Twin beds? What if we'd married our fathers, our mothers, our childhood pets? What if we'd projected or settled? What if we never had sex again?

"Don't be ridiculous," my new husband said as I repacked the unused peignoir set—peach thong and bra with push-up features—I'd so carefully selected. Ridiculous, exactly. If only I'd known that the lingerie bridal shower would turn out to be a practical joke, I'd have asked for appliances. I'd have never paraded around wearing that paper plate hat stapled high with bows. If only I'd known that the rites were expendable, I'd have skipped the embarrassment of the first dance and kept my bouquet. If only I'd known not to believe the age-old wedding-night hype that this would be my fantasy night.

"But how could you have known?" my new husband said. "It's not the kind of thing you read in magazines or books. Anyway, we have the honeymoon to make up for it, not to mention the rest of our lives." And so we did. And so we do.

How Insensitive
Paul Festa

Late in the summer of 2005, I visited a nondescript medical office in San Francisco's fog belt, lay down on an examination table, and had eleven regions of my penis poked by various gauges of monofilament. It wasn't quite what I'd envisioned when I'd signed up for the Penile Sensitivity Touch-Test Evaluation Study—"touch test" had conjured something a little sexier than a retired MD coming at me with medical-grade fishing line. But by the age of thirty-five, the human penis is nothing if not well schooled in disappointment, and so, for the good of science, I went through with the exam.

The science in this case concerned one of the most controversial and common medical procedures practiced in the West: circumcision of the penis. The study, published in the April 2007 *BJU International* (the former *British Journal of Urology*) under the title "Fine-Touch Pressure Thresholds in the Adult Penis," is the latest research salvo in the war for the neonatal foreskin.

Pro-circumcision forces have been getting the upper hand on the research front in recent months, brandishing high-profile studies associating male circumcision with significantly lower HIV-infection rates in Africa. And while the American Academy of Pediatrics continues to call the evidence "complex and conflicting," several older studies claim a link between male circumcision and lower rates of specific sexually transmitted diseases, including HIV, syphilis, and cancer of the sexual and reproductive organs.

Anti-circumcision advocates cite methodological problems with the STD studies while raising a separate question about the ethics of discarding a body part to prevent its becoming infected. In order to establish what, exactly, a male person loses when he loses his foreskin, the study set out to compare sensation in the cut and the uncut organ. Its conclusion may seem obvious to those of us with only a lay interest in the penis, but it's controversial, nonetheless: uncut dick feels more. A lot more.

"The study shows that the foreskin is the most sensitive portion of the penis," said study coauthor Robert Van Howe, a pediatrician at the Marquette General Health System in Marquette, Michigan. "It's not like you're chopping off plain old skin. The analogy would be like removing your lips, because the lips are more sensitive than the skin around them."

The study, organized by the anti-circumcision advocacy group NOCIRC (National Organization of Circumcision Information Resource Centers), isn't the first to compare the sensitivity of the cut and the uncut. Masters and Johnson found no difference between circumcised and uncircumcised men's glans sensitivity, but they didn't subject that finding to peer review. Another dozen studies cited in the *BJU International* report compared sexual function of cut and uncut men, and some looked—from an anatomical, rather than sensory, perspective—at the loss of sensory tissue in circumcision. But the study authors say they've achieved something new with their study: a comparative sensory mapping of the male organ.

This new cartography of the penis proffers nineteen zones. Missing from the circumcised male are eight of these penile destinations, four on the dorsal side (the outer prepuce, the orifice rim, the mucocutaneous junction, the ridged band) and four on the ventral (frenulum near ridged band, frenulum at mucocutaneous junction, orifice rim, and outer prepuce). Missing from the uncircumcised anatomy are two regions on this new map, and they're both scars.

In the areas that cut and uncut men have in common, the study showed a sensitivity deficit of between 2 and 33 percent. In those areas peculiar to the intact penis, the deficit is by definition 100 percent. And it's in those areas, the study concludes, where most of the sensory action is. Perhaps the most salient of the report's findings is that "the transitional region from the external to the internal prepuce is the most sensitive region of the uncircumcised penis and more sensitive than the most sensitive region of the circumcised penis." If the penile map were of New York City, the equivalent cut would be Manhattan from Fourteenth Street to Battery Park.

The genesis of the study was the day in May 1979 that nursing-school student Marilyn Milos witnessed a circumcision for the first time. Milos describes the experience on the NOCIRC website in excruciating detail: a newborn, strapped down spread-eagle on a plastic board, shrieking and wailing as his foreskin is clamped, incised, and finally amputated.

"I had not been prepared, nothing could have prepared me, for this experience," writes Milos, whose three sons were all circumcised before her stint in nursing school. "To see a part of this baby's penis being cut off—without an anesthetic—was devastating. But even more shocking was the doctor's comment, barely audible several octaves below the piercing screams of the baby, 'There's no medical reason for doing this.' "

Now Milos, the founder and executive director of NOCIRC, is a sixty-seven-year-old grandmother who proudly boasts of being thanked for her work by her "intact grandson—and his wife." Since her fateful afternoon in nursing school, says Milos, she has devoted every day of her life to bringing an end to what she describes as "an anachronistic blood ritual."

Harrowing narratives, many illustrated, are a staple of anti-circumcision websites, where doctors detail procedures gone awry and complain of poor documentation of the practice's true risks and consequences. (If parents had to do a Google Image search on "botched circumcision" before consenting to the procedure, its prevalence would surely plummet.)

Dispassionate analysis could sweep aside personal accounts like Milos' and dismiss accidental castrations, disfigurements, and deaths to the margin of error. After all, male circumcision is or has been routine in the United States for much of the last century, has been spiritually mandated among Jews for millennia, and the purported victims of this preputial pogrom are impregnating their wives and running the country and writing the very words before you. If there's a problem with snipping the foreskins of newborns, its manifestations are subtle.

I consider the fate of my own foreskin with ambivalence. Apart from bypassing a few Craigslist ads stating a preference for intact dick, I've never been aware of being discriminated against for lacking one. As a secular American Jew born in 1970, I've found myself for the most part in the company of men who were either ritually or routinely circumcised. While I take seriously the methodological qualms the anti-circumcision lobby raises about studies showing an

STD-foreskin link, that research at least jibes with my own experience, in which sexual contact with some unimaginable number of sex partners has yet to manifest so much as a pimple on my dick. (Coming of age at Ground Zero of both AIDS and condom awareness may also have something to do with it.) I've heard people complain that their intact partners were too quick to orgasm, or were so sensitive they could barely be touched by another person. These are problems I'm happy not to share. So what are we, what I'll call the silent and ambivalent circumcised majority, really missing?

Nothing, I tell myself. But then I remember those moments, so routine in my sex life I barely notice them, in which I'm supposed to be approaching orgasm and the goal seems a long, long way off; in which I jerk myself off until I'm chafed; in which I've run my hands through the hair of someone giving me what has every appearance of being a splendid blowjob and yet I am detached from the experience. And I am detached for the reason that I just don't feel it very much. The thought occurs to me that we who lost the most sensitive parts of our sexual organ to a ritual or routine procedure in the first days of life are detached and apathetic and ambivalent because we do not know what we are missing.

The Study of Sex
Amy André

In a large classroom packed with students, Professor Nick Baham is teaching a course called African-American Sexuality. The course has been taught in the Ethnic Studies Department of California State University, East Bay since the mid-'80s, with Baham taking over as professor in 2000. The students settle in as he turns their attention to a guest lecturer, who is visiting to discuss images of people of color in feminist pornography.

Most of the students in the class are themselves black and mostly female. They range in age from late twenties to early thirties, and between fifty and sixty people take the class when it's offered several times a year. Most students identify as heterosexual. As far as Baham knows, it is the only course in the country specifically on African-American sexuality. For today's lecture, Baham and his guest field questions about black female sexual agency, the involvement of black people in alternative sexual communities and even representations of pleasure and orgasm.

Contrary to some students' expectations, the ten-week course is not a sexual "how-to." Baham's challenge is to get students to step out of their comfort zones, as they cover topics such as BDSM, black LGBT issues, sex work, media hype around the "down low," marketing of black female bodies on television, representations of black sexuality in pornography, interracial sexuality, and black male patriarchy.

Rethinking What's Natural

Students enroll in the course with a variety of ideas about sexuality, Baham says. Among his students, he finds that "certain things are considered taboo because they're considered things that white people do. For example, gay and lesbian identity is considered white, introduced to blacks during slavery and not organic to Africa. Religiosity also comes up; sexual practice is conflated with religious prerogatives."

Representations of black sexuality, especially black female sexuality, in popular culture are also an issue. "They're very aware that their sexual bodies are objectified and commodified," Baham says. "And there are clearly demarcated lines between [women who are] virgins and sluts. [The students'] sexual self-perception is bounded by race, gender, and religiosity. Every erotic activity that they're engaged in becomes a contested cultural terrain, where [they're] fighting the legacy of colonialism."

For one of the class assignments, Baham has the students conduct a mini-ethnography. He asks students to interview people whose sexuality is different from that of their own. "So, if they're heterosexual and vanilla, they go to the Folsom Street Fair (an annual leather community event in the nearby city of San Francisco) and chat with people," he says.

"I'm not trying to indoctrinate them. I'm not trying to stop them from looking to the Christian church every time they have sex. I'm looking to get them to think critically about what they do and what they think is 'natural.' "

The Color of Sexuality Studies

The existence of Baham's course itself—and its high enrollment numbers—indicates a departure from the norm in the field of sexuality studies. Rita Melendez is a professor in the Human Sexuality Studies Department at San Francisco State University and a research associate at the school's Center for Research on Gender and Sexuality. Both at sexuality studies conferences and in her own classroom, she often finds that she is one of a handful of people of color. Most of her colleagues are white, as are most of her students.

The field of sexuality studies is small but growing, having emerged from an interdisciplinary social sciences arena. Academics and theorists dating back to Freud popularized the notion of studying human sexual behavior, and its development has been shaped by everything from the early psychologists to the birth of feminist theory, from the advent of HIV/AIDS to the creation of women's and gender studies, and more.

Melendez contends that "when you study sexuality, race and ethnicity are pivot points. Who you study and what you find will be influenced by race. There needs to be a lot more people of color doing sexuality studies." Sexuality studies has immediate relevance to communities of color, she argues, because of historical and contemporary intersections between sexualized racism and racialized sexism, and because of the ways in which sexuality can be a particular source of joy for persons of color as well.

Race "hasn't been dealt with very well" in sexuality studies,

Melendez says. Despite the fact that many people of color are interested in the topic, "there has been mainly a large group of white men and women in the field of sexuality. A lot has to do with the word 'sexuality'; it gets associated with white people." Melendez finds that when the word "sexuality" gets added to a course title, people of color don't enroll.

Part of that word-association has to do with the fact that many white sexuality researchers are researching people of color. For example, Melendez says, most research being done today on people with HIV is done on people of color with HIV. For that reason, a notion prevails that sexuality studies is something that white people do and something that people of color have done to them. This paradigm sets up a power dynamic that can leave people of color dissociated from the sexuality research field.

Another reason for the low numbers of students of color in sexuality studies courses may have to do with the way race plays out in the mostly white classroom. "I spend all day talking about sexuality. I can say anything in my classes, and nobody will be shocked. But when [I] start talking about race, it often becomes a sensitive subject for my students," Melendez says. "When we really start talking about what race means, we get uncomfortable. Students tend to think that if you know somebody's race, you know a lot about them. I think that's not true. Everybody experiences race and ethnicity differently. If you're white, does that mean we can presume to know everything about you? It's really important to de-teach [my sexuality studies students] about race. [I] constantly try to bring race and ethnicity into the conversation."

When she was in graduate school at Columbia University in 2002, Melendez witnessed firsthand the degree to which many other people of color share her interest in sexuality studies. She was involved in the development of a program at Columbia called

MOSAIC, which was intended to get undergraduate students of color involved in the field. By offering minischolarships, conducting weekly seminars, and bringing the students to conferences such as the ones held by the Society for the Scientific Study of Sexuality (a leading national sexuality studies organization), MOSAIC was able to engage students of color and legitimize their preexisting interest in sexuality studies.

Melendez believes that sexuality studies needs to embrace students of color by creating more structural programs, like MOSAIC, and more courses that acknowledge and examine the intersections of race and sexuality, like Baham's African-American Sexuality. "It's vital that more people of color enter the field, but I don't think that's going to happen until people make a concerted effort." This effort, she says, could include sexuality studies programs working to get more students of color into their classes; it could also entail black or other ethnic studies programs including classes on sexuality in their roster, and it could mean an academy-wide effort to destigmatize the word "sexuality" itself.

Race, Sex, and Power

Baham's time in the classroom goes a long way toward meeting all three of those goals. But the real revolution comes from within.

At the beginning of the course, Baham says, students always come in with a "pseudo-scientific" notion. "The question that they want answered is: Why are people gay?" Baham says. "I get them to understand that asking 'why' comes from a particular privileged position of power," namely that of heteronormativity.

Baham also gets the students to look at the notion "that black gay men are the biggest health risk in the black community. What about cocaine, heroin, unsafe sex among heterosexuals?" In getting students to critically examine topics such as internalized and externalized homophobia, Baham encourages analysis of the ways in which students personally construct their own sexualities.

Finally, the course ends with a look at BDSM. "We've had this motif that runs through the course: it's called power," Baham says. "I ask the students: How about if we play with power? How about if we play with violence? How about if we play with slavery? I talk about BDSM as a political act. [In BDSM], all the issues with gender roles, slavery, violence and power, all of these come to a head. I deal with it as a potentially very mature way for people to resolve issues that develop from the sexual persona, such as pain, loss, mistrust."

Baham starts by talking about spanking or being spanked as an example of what BDSM can entail. He'll often bring in a guest speaker from the BDSM community. Through these discussions, the students are able to see the potential for BDSM to be, as he puts it, "a redemptive and spiritual act." His students often mention having a slight interest in the topic, but that they don't know what it is and think that it's a "white thing." Despite this, students report that the idea of "doing things that are aggressive or submissive is exciting. There's a tremendous amount of interest, but real lack of information on it," Baham says. "When I talk about trust and safewords, and they see it's not people getting together willy-nilly and beating the crap out of each other, they can understand it. Only later do we talk about the more extreme forms of BDSM, such as race play."

Baham often overhears his students telling their friends, "Man, you wouldn't believe what we do in that class!"—which he takes as a compliment.

What does the future hold for Baham's African-American Sexuality and for Melendez' desire to see more people of color studying and researching sexuality? In CSU East Bay's Ethnic Studies Department, Baham and colleague Luz Calvo have proposed the creation of an entire departmental program to focus on the gender and sexuality of people of color. The African-American Sexuality course would become part of that program along with similar courses.

Melendez dreams of the day when academics will work to make sure that "young people of color know the importance of studying sexuality, that it's not just fun and games, but that it deals with really important issues that are of concern to many communities of color" such as HIV/ AIDS, intimate partner violence, pregnancy and birth control, the rights of same-gender-loving individuals, and sexual agency and the right to pleasurable experiences. "If I had my way," she concludes, "sexuality studies would take over the entire university, because everything relates to sexuality."

Dangerous Dildos
Tristan Taormino

Many years ago, I did a photo shoot with porn star Chloe for *Taboo* magazine. It had been a long day of a hundred different poses and we were tired. "Let's get that double dong and do an ass-to-ass shot," said the photographer right before her assistant handed me a red two-headed rubber dildo fresh out of its package, with that shiny film on it that many jelly toys have. I spread lube on one end and began to slide the dildo into my ass, which was already warmed up from Chloe's fingers. As the head slipped inside, my ass suddenly felt like it was on fire. A burning sensation spread throughout my butt, and when I looked up at Chloe, who was waiting for her end, she said, "I know that look. The toy must be old. Hot poker, right?" I yanked the fiery phallus out and jetted to the ladies room where I used an enema bottle filled with warm water to rinse out my butt. It didn't do much good. I would later learn that the culprit was phthalates, a group of industrial chemicals with many uses, including, as I found out, being a pain in the ass.

Phthalates (the *ph* is silent) are added to polyvinyl chloride (PVC) to make it more pliable, so they are often found in soft plastic things, like toys made for small children, animals, and sexual pleasure. Vinyl sex toys containing the chemicals are among the most inexpensive and widely available on the market. But while their texture makes them ideal for insertables, it turns out that what makes them enjoyable may also make them toxic. Because phthalate-spiked PVC is not a stable inert compound, these toys continually leach phthalates, which can cause a nasty odor, a greasy film, and genital irritation (like the burning sensation in my ass?).

It seems like phthalates are everywhere: they're in cosmetics, perfume, hair products, body lotion, deodorant, nail polish, carpeting, flooring tile, and medical devices. But that's not all: A 2000 National Institutes of Health (NIH) study concluded that 85 to 90 percent of our phthalate exposure comes from food—mainly meat and fish. They come from processing equipment and food packaging, and because they're everywhere in the environment, they've made their way into the food chain. Today, you probably washed some down the drain.

In studies on mice and rats, high levels of phthalates have been linked to reproductive organ damage, liver damage, and liver cancer. According to Consumer Reports, four studies published in the NIH journal *Environmental Health Perspectives* have linked high phthalate levels to human health issues, including premature breast development in young girls, low sperm count or motility in men, and lower testosterone levels in male newborns. The most well-publicized human study tested the urine of pregnant women and found that a higher level of phthalates correlated with a smaller anogenital index (the distance between the anus and the genitals) in male newborns. However, critics argue that the science of the study is flawed and there's no evidence that being on the small end of the anogenital index is problematic.

Other countries have responded to the potential threat based on rodent studies and research. In 1998, Canada took children's rattles, teethers, and dog chew-toys made with phthalates off the shelves. In 2005, after an eight-year battle, the European Union banned the use of three phthalates in children's toys and child-care products and the use of three others in toys and items that can be put in children's mouths. According to Environmental Science and Technology Online, "Some disagreement existed over the risk assessments....The technical experts concluded that DINP, the phthalate most widely used in toys, posed no risk. However, the Scientific Committee for Toxicity, Ecotoxicity and the Environment disagreed and considered it a potential risk. The Environment Directorate of the European Commission advised the EP [European Parliament] that enough 'scientific uncertainty' existed to warrant limiting the use of DINP in toys that can be sucked and chewed." The U.S. Consumer Product Safety Commission (CPSC) tested similar products and concluded they are not harmful. But if Canadian and European kids can't put such products in their pie-holes, should we be sliding them into other holes?

There have only been two studies on the relationship between sex toys and phthalates, both European. In September 2006, the Danish Technological Institute's "Analysis and Health Risk Assessment of Chemical Substances in Sex Toys" concluded that implied health risks were minor to nonexistent (except for pregnant and breast-feeding women, who were cautioned against "heavy usage"). In the same month, Dutch research firm TNO (hired by Greenpeace Netherlands) found that seven of the eight toys it tested contained at least one of the phthalates banned by the EU, and that phthalates made up 24 to 49 percent of the toys' composition.

Although the study didn't contain any new information about the health effects, Greenpeace called for the ban of sex toys containing phthalates.

Researching the research on phthalates is a dizzying project in itself, with each side of the argument using scientific jargon to discredit the other. Environmental activists say they're toxic and should be banned. The Environmental Protection Agency classifies one phthalate (DEHP) as a probable human carcinogen (based on the rodent studies). Right on cue, the plastics industry, its lobbyists, and the CPSC insist that phthalates are proven safe. Then there are the unbiased number crunchers: Statistical Assessment Service (STATS), a group which analyzes "the use and abuse of science and statistics in the media" (see stats.org) concludes, "The phthalate story is a complicated one.... There is evidence that our exposure level is about 1000 times lower than the level of exposure at which rats display observable effects. However, since primates are different from rats, we cannot conclude that phthalates are either safe or unsafe based on the animal studies." But Trevor Butterworth of STATS says, "This is not a public health crisis."

So what's a tree-hugging dildo-loving girl to do? Mine is not an isolated incident; ask any sex store clerk or porn star: lots of people are talking about the burning, itching, and other irritation experienced after using PVC sex toys with phthalates.

Another downside to these toys is that they're porous, so they cannot be easily cleaned or completely disinfected (like nonporous materials such as silicone or glass). Irritation is one thing, but whether these toys are toxic and cause long-term problems is a hotly debated question. The research cited above has shown a link between the chemicals and cancer in mice and rats but not in humans. (Furthermore, most human research deals with phthalate exposure through the skin and mouth, not through the absorbent tissue of the genitals.) What *is* clear is that the issue highlights a growing tension within the sex toy industry between companies stuck in an outdated "adult novelty" model and those invested in raising the bar.

When co-owner Jessica Giordani opened the Smitten Kitten, a sex toy shop in Minneapolis, her first shipment of PVC toys arrived in a box with a strong odor and full of what looked like oil stains. According to Giordani, when she questioned her distributor about it, he said, "Oh, yeah, that happens." Unsatisfied with that answer, she asked the manufacturers about their ingredients. No one would tell her what their toys were made of. So, Giordani decided to do the research herself, which led to the formation of CATT, the Coalition Against Toxic Toys (badvibes.org), a nonprofit consumer advocacy and education organization dedicated to ending the manufacture, distribution, and retail sale of toxic sex toys. CATT sends popular toys (like the Rabbit Habit) to an independent lab to test their formulations and publishes the findings on its website. "We want to make the information available to consumers so they can make informed decisions," says Giordani. The Smitten Kitten and Womyn's Ware in Canada won't carry any toy they consider toxic. Other retail stores, like Good Vibrations and Babeland, inform customers what a toy is made of, and, in the case of toys with phthalates, recommend using a condom over them.

Thanks to Giordani and others, there's been enough media coverage about the issue and dialogue among retailers and consumers that many toy manufacturers have begun advertising products as "phthalate-free." This would seem like a step in the right direction; however, unlike other products, sex toys are not regulated by any agency (part of this is due to an unfortunate loophole whereby sex toys are labeled "for novelty use" meaning they have no actual use). The FDA makes sure that shampoo manufacturers must tell you what's in their product, but dildo companies are not required to list a toy's actual ingredients. This allows the industry to provide misleading and incorrect labeling, which it routinely does, from "hypoallergenic dildos" to so-called silicone toys that aren't made of silicone. Some well-established companies recognize the need for change and have moved toward higher quality products; others don't seem that concerned.

When you look at the phthalate issue in a larger context, what you see is the current split within the sex toy industry between old-school adult novelty makers and new age sex-positive toy companies. The former are stuck in a model of "get it as cheap as you can from China, make it look like a penis (that's what women want, right?), and spend as little as you can on packaging." Toys from these companies scream, "Who cares if this looks good or actually works? No one's going to return it or complain, they'll be too embarrassed. Besides, it's just a dildo," reinforcing people's low expectations and shame. Nick Orlandino, chief operating officer of Pipedream Products, recently told *Adult Novelty Business,* "Most of our customers don't give a shit what their toy is made of." This gag-gift mentality treats its products, and by extension sexual pleasure and satisfaction, as frivolous and unimportant.

Metis Black, president of silicone toy manufacturer Tantus (tantusinc.com), disagrees with this attitude: "Consumers need to expect more and demand higher quality products." Tantus toys are made of the highest quality (and most expensive) medical-grade platinum silicone. Black thinks there should be self-regulation within the toy industry and transparency when it comes to the ingredients they use. "The phthalate studies are a mixed bag. We know that these toys smell and off-gas, and that can't be good for you. It's not just phthalates. They've found cadmium and lead and industrial-grade mineral oil, which is like kerosene, in some toys."

Tantus is part of a new generation of companies dedicated to research and development, top-quality materials, attention to detail, and consumer satisfaction. These sex-positive manufacturers design and test their products with real bodies and pleasure in mind. They stand behind their stuff, and want consumers to know they have the right to toys that are well made, long lasting, and do what they say they'll do. They treat butt plugs like they treat sex: as something valued and valuable.

As these two kinds of companies with radically different philosophies battle for a share of the market, I can only hope that quality will prevail over making a fast buck. My pussy and ass deserve quality sex toys. So do yours.

Absolut Nude
Miriam Datskovsky

Naked parties are bullshit.

Yet nude living, especially the naked party—also known, in my humble opinion, as grunting, sweating bodies unnecessarily sacrificing sexual pleasure—has taken off at college campuses nationwide. Naked parties are an established underground trend at Brown, Yale, Northwestern, and Pomona. At Wesleyan, one of the dormitories, West College, also known as WestCo, is affectionately nicknamed the Naked Dorm—clothing is optional. Hamilton College even has its own self-proclaimed "varsity streaking team," a group of students who can be seen tiptoeing through libraries and running down hills in flying-*V* formation while making *caw* noises, stark naked. They consider themselves number one in the nation.

Columbia, too, has joined the naked ranks. The annual naked run never fails to draw a large, excited crowd. Lingerie and full-on naked parties are becoming increasingly common. Carla Bloomberg, de facto Columbia naked party spokeswoman, featured in both *New York* magazine and the *New York Sun,* has repeatedly insisted that naked parties are not about sex. Instead, she claims they are about challenging social constructs, and more specifically, the idea that we define ourselves by what we wear.

Carla has a point. I'll be the first to confess: I am obsessed, down to the matching earrings and stilettos, with my clothes. But stripping down to your birthday suit at a designated naked party is not the same as doing so in front of a lover. In some sense, naked parties are simply another social construct: if everyone is naked, then people are likely to feel comfortable about it, and everyone can easily agree that being naked is supremely better than being clothed. And while it might be easier to pinpoint how people spend hours perfecting their outfits in order to refine their self-images, that does not preclude those people who spend hours working out, perfecting their body images so they will look and feel sexually attractive without their clothes on.

Still, defying or creating social constructs aside, I'm not convinced it is possible to think about nudity without thinking about sex. Like it or not, some wack combination of hormones and neurotransmitters that my humanities-inclined mind refuses to comprehend automatically goes off whenever we see someone we are even remotely attracted to in the nude. Boobs. Penis. Sex. Simple, really.

So what is it about nudity that makes us feel so, well, naked?

"Nudity," actress Bridget Fonda once declared, "is who people are at the most interesting part of the evening, when they take off their protective layer, when no one is watching." If this is the case, then I have been missing out. The physical specificities of my lovers tend to take a backseat to more important matters, e.g., sexual positions and continuous orgasms. I have zero desire to think about his patchy chest hair or nonexistent abs, much less how my stomach and thighs must look without clothes to hide under. Grunting, sweating bodies are best ignored in favor of assured, maximized sexual pleasure.

So much of our discomfort with nudity has to do with environment and social convention. At the beach, people feel comfortable in bikinis and Speedos, but not bras and boxers, largely because walking around in your bathing suit, even it means you are effectively nude, is socially acceptable. Walking around in your underwear is not. Same goes for locker rooms—walking around naked after a workout has little significance. Undressing someone in bed for the first time, even if you've already seen him or her naked in the locker room, takes on an entirely different meaning.

Maybe it gets difficult when someone we care about is watching us. Our vulnerability levels skyrocket. Going to a naked party with a bunch of random people is much easier—who cares what people you don't know think? Going to a naked party with your lover is an entirely different, excuse the pun, ball game. So is going with a close friend, for that matter. We're much more sensitive about our self-images when we care about the person (or people) observing us.

Genuine examine-every-crevice-in-my-body-and-fuck-me-with-the-lights-on nudity can be equally, if not more, erotic than sexual intercourse in and of itself. Which means it takes guts. If sex marks the shift in a relationship from friendship to something more, then nudity, in its rawest form, marks a relationship's shift from something more to something that can't be taken any further. To the normal human eye, the most you can observe about a person is visible when he or she is naked. Even for the most serious of couples, there is nothing more to see, nothing more to explore.

Everything, including those physical attributes you like least about yourself and your lover, is suddenly on the table.

But it is not just more erotic, it is more intimate. About as intimate as it gets. Because once you are mutually raw and naked with someone, you'll never look at that person the same way again.

The Hung List
Scott Poulson-Bryant

In an industry that prizes the very thing that, symbolically, keeps a Denzel Washington off the hung list—the looming possibility that he hangs better and is just waiting to unleash that hangature on the world—Lexington Steele is a bona fide leading man. In an industry in which women are the main attraction, in which female faces (and other body parts) are the selling points that move product, Steele is a star. With his massive fan following and record-setting three Best Male Performer awards from the *Adult Video News* (a sort of porn version of *Variety*-meets-the Academy of Motion Picture Arts and Sciences), compared to other men in the porn biz who are mainly, mostly, studs for hire, Steele reigns supreme. He is a tall, pitch-perfect evocation of what singer India.Arie affectionately calls "Brown Skin." He is also a perfect evocation of that love-cum-envy that Toni Morrison's *Sula* detailed so incisively—because, to put it bluntly, Steele is not only model handsome and athletically built, he is also hung, very well hung. Lexington Steele is eleven inches long. Eleven-by-seven-inches hung.

On the list of brothers in porn's unofficial Beyond Ten Club, Lexington is said to come second, after Jack Napier, and before Sean Michaels, Jake Steed, Byron Long, and Justin Slayer. He may come second on that list, but if you ask around, many porn aficionados will rank Steele higher, partly because of his superior bedside manner and partly because, when compared to the other guys in the porn business, he is the whole package. Steele can pull it off, no pun intended. "It" being the ability to perform, which in the world of porn is more than whipping out the dick and stuffing it wherever the director instructs it to be stuffed. "It" is that highly regarded ability to be hard on cue (reportedly less stressful lately with the advent of Viagra), to be ready to shoot—in both senses of the word—when the director is ready to film, to be able to act the scene and make it real for the audience.

As provocative as a big dick might seem to us laypeople, size isn't always what gets a guy into the porn game. "Size almost pales next to performance," Steele told me one August night. "Next to the ability to shoot on cue or last longer to make a scene work? A big dick might get you in the door, but that ability to really perform is what keeps you in the game."

That ability to perform well has made Lexington Steele more than one of the most popular porn actors to successfully make the transition to director/producer/owner. With Mercenary Pictures, the production company he founded in 2002, Steele has some control over his image and how his films get produced and distributed. Though he's had success performing as the Impaler in a series of films, appearing in the *Up Your Ass* series and guest starring in Jake Steed's mega-successful *Little White Chicks and Big Black Monster Dicks* franchise, Steele has given the world under the Mercenary banner *Lex Steele XXX, Black Reign, Top Guns, Super Whores,* and *Lex on Blondes.* His triple-threat status as performer/producer/director doesn't just make him a brand name to be reckoned with; it also provides him with a clever and clear-eyed way of looking at the business of porn. When he told me, "This is a business and as a performer you look to penetrate a market," it is clear that he appreciates the intended pun and appreciates that I appreciate it. "You also look to maximize your potential as a brand. You know that you're filling a void and that you're giving the audience a fantasy, but that doesn't mean that I'm not aware of what it means that I do what I do."

That awareness might come from the unusual way he made his way to porn. Before Lexington Steele was Lexington Steele, a king of West Coast porn production, he was a suburban East Coast kid, from Morristown, New Jersey, a middle-class, churchgoing kid who didn't have girlfriends but excelled at sports (and lettered in three) before graduating from high school and first matriculating at Morehouse College only to eventually transfer to Syracuse. No girlfriends? "This was the late eighties, early nineties," he told me. "It was all about the light-skinned, curly-haired brothers. The world wasn't safe for the shaved-head dark brother yet."

After college, where he pledged the black fraternity Omega Psi Phi, the stereotypically rowdier-than-thou Q-Dogs, Steele took his degree and landed on Wall Street, trading stocks and bonds for Oppenheimer. He did some modeling, the "legit" kind with his clothes on, but that didn't last. He was, simply, too big for the sample-sized clothes models were expected to sell to buyers and shoppers on the runways and in the photo shoots. Not too big down there, but in his broad shoulders and long legs. Someone suggested that he try modeling for some adult publications and those jobs led to the suggestion that he try his hand at the porn biz. Which certainly was a place he'd never hear that he was "too big" for anything. So, in 1998, with enough money saved to last him, he figured, three or four months, he headed west, and there he remains.

His first few jobs, as it is for black dudes arriving on the scene, were primarily in all-black productions, doing sex scenes with black women. But he wanted to move into the interracial market, mainly because it paid more money and could only broaden his audience. And, like he'd told me, he was aware of what he was doing and, most important, aware of what was needed of him. "White consumers have certain expectations," he told me. "The idea of the big black buck deflowering the little virginal white girl is very popular." Steele could do the "deflowering" but he also learned that as much as the audience may enjoy that scene, there was an irony at work that didn't completely surprise him. To "deflower the little virginal white girls," producers hired a specific sort of black man. This was the other part of the package: along with the big dick and the ability to "perform," Steele, like other black guys who wanted to work the lucrative interracial market, had to be what he calls "palatable." "Nonthreatening," he told me.

Interesting concept: black men hired to be the big black buck had to be nonthreatening and palatable enough to appeal to the white men who wanted to jerk off to images of little virginal white girls being deflowered. In other words, they wanted their big black bucks not to be too black.

Just black enough, one supposes, to fuck a white girl.

According to Pat Riley, a pornography expert who posts rants and raves about the industry on his porn info site RAME (rame. net), "for the longest time,"

The porn industry... [traded] in the most pejorative views of blacks it [could] find. Pornographers perpetuate the stereotypical view of a shiftless, maladjusted group. [Racism in porn] is not some white actress who doesn't want to screw a black guy (for whatever reason) but a concerted attempt by the producers to appeal to the basest elements of the viewing population.

But then there was the porn-era post-Sean Michaels, an articulate, bespectacled, briefcase-carrying black stud who played scenes as if he was a black Gregory Peck with a ten-inch dick running down the leg of his boxers underneath his gray flannel suit. Sean had single-handedly changed the rules for brothers in the porn game. Not only was he "palatable" but he was smarter than the average stud, more sophisticated than the average viewer, a tall ebony-skinned Adonis who never soiled his white collar.

"Sean paved the way for me," Steele told me. "All roads lead back to Sean Michaels and what he did for the image of the black guy in porn." Essentially Michaels had retrieved the tropes of standard white-boy professionalism and flipped it into a sort of sexy pose of black-boy cool. So you had to be just black enough (and hung big) to fuck a white girl, but not so threatening that you scare her in the parking lot after the shoot.

According to Steele, his video releases sell like, well, hotcakes. Whereas most porn videos will move approximately three thousand or so pieces upon initial release, then trail off at about five thousand copies over the next six months, Steele's titles such as *Heavy Metal, Volumes 1* and *2,* will move five thousand copies upon release. Others have moved up to seven thousand pieces upon release and move about ten thousand copies in the next three months. These are major numbers in the porn market. And at twelve dollars a pop, that's quite a few coins for an entrepreneurial porn actor to jangle in his pocket.

Lexington Steele, college-educated former Wall Street broker, works in a business where strangers fuck strangers for money, where the big black beast is an accepted role to be played in a public space, for a huge fan base of black men who worship him as the sexual superhero that he portrays on-screen and white men who want to see Steele whipping out his big black monster dick and ferociously putting it to a tiny white girl. Steele feels the sexual sting of stereotyping every day he goes to work: as the hung black stud he's the personification of a stereotype that controls the very image of black men everywhere, yet he has to rely on the stereotype as a fantasy creation to ensure that he stays on top of his game. Steele laughs as he recounts this, mostly, it seems, because he realizes the utter paradox of it—culturally and economically speaking.

"By nature," Steele says, "this business isn't about any color except green—money. I mean, the only thing that separates it from being prostitution is that there's a camera in the room when people are doing their thing." As a producer, as someone who hires and fires talent every day, Steele has a fairly sanguine approach to it all, particularly coming up against the casting of white women and the usual conflicts that arise around that issue. "I don't have a problem with hiring white girls who want to work. I'm seeing product. My own films don't have a color line. All races are represented in the scenes. However if you allow my brown skin to overshadow my green money, then fuck you, that's your loss."

Not that this behavior is limited to the stars of the business. "I've met girls fresh off the bus from West Virginia or Utah, coming into this business and immediately stating that they don't do black guys. This from a girl who's probably fucked her way across the country to get here, who wants to make a living fucking strangers on camera. She'll fuck for money, she won't do it with a black dude." He laughs off such a contradiction because he also knows there's a secret buried in that paradox—as there usually is when race and sex meet for a little session. "The thing is," he told me, "that many, many of these girls who 'won't screw a black guy' really mean that they won't screw a black guy on-screen. I know of a few of these women who do private shows with black guys. Let some rapper call, or some basketball player ring up and say he wants to get down. Then let's see these females talk about 'not screwing black guys.' "

"I take the good with the bad," he added. "Of course there're elements to doing this that doesn't necessarily add up. It can be both emasculating as well as empowering." Emasculating because "you know you're the animal phallus, the beast. I know that I'm dealt with for what's between my legs, but at the same time, there's something to being cherished, to being the desired one even as you know you're filling a stereotype."

Said by the man who looked to the hip-hop music industry and World Wrestling Federation to find a way of crafting a branded image for himself. "You know how rappers and wrestlers are like characters?" he told me. "That's my model. Method Man can be Johnny Blaze or whoever else. I can be the Impaler, the Dark Prince, the Black Viking."

He's the guy who is the soft-spoken cat, opening the first installment of *Heavy Metal* by inviting a journalist into his home to interview him, then modestly pulling out his eleven-inch dick when she asks to see it, telling her that it's not even the biggest one in the porn biz. He's the guy who ends his time with me quoting Dr. Frances Cress Welsing, a noted theorist on race. Welsing has a theory about color, about how it is color itself—before you even get to the invented tropes of stereotypes and myths—that intimidates people, that the sheer appearance of black or brown skin is the perceived salvo in the waged war of race hatred that has plagued human relations.

War, indeed. The first *Little White Chicks and Big Monster Dicks*

(1999) opens with a disclaimer that the filmmaker (Jake Steed) doesn't mean to attack any racial group. But it certainly can't be an accident that the director/producer of the video—billed as a Jake Steed Production—is credited as A. Trublackman. Jake Steed: a True Black Man, Who's Hung Like a Horse.

The black male body is, I've decided, something like American history's Trojan horse, hiding in plain sight, invisible as its real self yet highly visible as its mythical self, a hopefully benign gift unwrapped to expose a seething mass of warring contradictions, the enemy in the midst. Perhaps porn is the place that expresses this better than anything.

Maybe the phrase should be hung like a Trojan horse.

The Glass Closet
Michael Musto

"Bravo, Jodie Foster!" That cry has long sounded among easily charmed gay celebrity watchers from Hollywood to Gotham. After all, Jodie is one of the original out-but-not-really-out queens of "at least." You know: She's never come out publicly, but at least she's never tried to claim she's straight either. She's talked incessantly about her kids, but at least she hasn't named the father and tried to make it sound like he was any kind of love interest. She won her greatest acclaim for a movie protested by gay activists—*The Silence of the Lambs*—and reportedly refused to do a short film based on the lesbian classic *Rubyfruit Jungle*, but at least she isn't afraid to play tough women, single moms, and parts originally written for men (even if that might be what she mostly gets offered).

And though her '92 Oscar speech for *Lambs* seemed to confirm her tenacious belief in the semicloset ("I'd like to thank all the people in this industry who have respected my choices and who have not been afraid of the power and the dignity that entitles me to"), at least she's never threatened lawsuits when press people drag her out of it!

By all reports, Jodie lives an out life—within serious limits— while cagily avoiding any on-the-record revelations, a delicate dance that's difficult to pull off—but not nearly so much so as double-bolting the door and living a total lie. Jodie, it turns out, is one of the foremost residents of a glass closet—that complex but popular contraption that allows public figures to avoid the career repercussions of any personal disclosure while living their lives with a certain degree of integrity. Such a device enables the public to see right in while not allowing them to actually open the latch unless the celebrity eventually decides to do so herself.

The glass closet is nothing new in Hollywood. Back in the 1920s and '30s, leading man William Haines was gay in everything except magazine interviews. (He was, in fact, as gay as any star was allowed to be in that era, and when he crossed the line—getting arrested in a gay incident and then refusing to hook up in a fake marriage—his acting career was kaput.) In the '70s performers like Paul Lynde and post-Liza Peter Allen similarly went as far as seemed possible, hinting around at their sexuality and even making appearances at various gay spots. But they could be certain the squeamish media wouldn't push things any further by addressing that, so they remained flamboyantly, ambiguously glassed off. And today, the press still gives a free pass to people like "Good Morning America" weather anchor Sam Champion and CNN presence Anderson Cooper, helping to keep their glass doors shut so they can lead gay social lives while carefully skirting the issue. The media has a field day with all kinds of oddballs, but the earnest TV-news presences—whom everyone has a crush on—get "protected," even though Cooper has been seen in gay bars in New York and

Champion sightings have long been reported from Fire Island to the Roxy.

The glass closet seems to make a perfect fit for a lot of celebs today, when gay is inching toward becoming more okay in the entertainment world. In an increasingly gay-tolerant environment, these stars can enjoy actual relationships, they don't have to constantly dredge up opposite-sex dates (other than their mothers), and after a day of pretending for the cameras they can go back to almost being themselves.

But at the same time, the stars aren't willing to make the jump to being officially labeled queer and all that it represents in the business. Douglas Carter Beane's timely play *The Little Dog Laughed*—which ran earlier this season on Broadway—had a wily lesbian agent, Diane, not only angling to heterosexualize her client's breakthrough movie role but trying to do the same thing to the client himself. I wasn't surprised to read at least one review that seemed to think Diane was a winsomely heroic "fairy godmother"!

She was more like a Machiavellian deception queen who's terrified of shattered glass, though some closet-busting survivors might say she had a point. In his memoir, *Red Carpets and Other Banana Skins*, Rupert Everett describes losing jobs in *About a Boy* and *Basic Instinct 2* specifically because he's openly gay. (And no, in the latter case, he probably didn't dodge a bullet. A quality art-house director was set to helm it at that point.)

What's more, Everett deserved an Oscar nomination for *My Best Friend's Wedding*, but the Academy generally frowns on out gays playing gays—it's not really acting, after all. Though Sir Ian McKellen broke the curse in 1999 with a Best Actor nomination for *Gods and Monsters*, actual trophies have been reserved for "courageous" straights playing gay, like William Hurt, Tom Hanks, Hilary Swank, Charlize Theron, and Philip Seymour Hoffman (as if it takes

courage to accept career-defining roles most actors would die for).
Alas, whenever another X-Men movie rolls around, no one says,
"Wow, Sir Ian was so brave to play straight! What a stretch!"

"I think there are four kinds of gays in Hollywood," explains
Howard Bragman, CEO of the PR firm Fifteen Minutes. "There's
the openly gay; the gay and everybody knows it but nobody talks
about it; the married, closeted gay who doesn't talk about it; and
the screaming 'I'll sue you if you say I'm gay' person." In other
words, the no closet, the glass closet, the cast iron closet, and the
closet you get buried in.

In the case of the Windex people, says Bragman, "A lot of actors
are afraid of being defined by their sexuality. In Hollywood they
don't cast by positives, they cast by negatives: 'This one's too this
or that.' And actors don't want to give red flags. They're actors and
want to talk about their mutability, not their personal lives." (Except
for their adorable children, their busy workload that precludes any
relationships, and their utter admiration for Kylie Minogue.)

These glass-housed actors, he adds, "are comfortable with their
decision because they feel like they're living honestly." But if someone who's struggling with the sexuality issue comes to Bragman,
he'll advise him or her to totally come out. "Their career may be
different and less lucrative," he says, "but everyone I've seen come
out has been happier as a result of it." Of course, in Hollywood
"less lucrative" and "happier" don't generally appear in the same
sentence.

Bragman handled the coming-out campaign for former NBA
star John Amaechi, who Bragman says has lived openly but never
came out publicly because it would have thrown the team balance
off-kilter in the same way a straight headline-grabber like a divorce
does. But the basketball star is now retired and promoting his new
book, *Man in the Middle*, so the glass is no longer required.

In a phone interview the U.K.-raised Amaechi—who played for the Orlando Magic and Utah Jazz and now works as a psychologist—explains to me his longtime lifestyle. "I was a regular at gay places on the road," he says, "from WeHo to [the New York City bar] Splash. It's not as if I was hiding." And he'd bring gay friends—and even a partner once—to the backstage area where his teammates would invite their wives and girlfriends. What's more, he says, "If someone asked me if I was gay, I'd either joke and say, 'You're not pretty enough. You've got nothing to worry about,' or I'd tell the truth. I never lied. I even told a reporter once, but he didn't report it." Through much of the '90s the "Peter Allen free pass" was still in full operation across the boards.

But why stay covered in glass and not come out even more openly back then? "I talked to people about it—my friends, mostly," Amaechi says. "Some suggested it was a very good idea to not come out. I was worried about my career and what it would be like walking through stadiums. In thirty states I could still have been fired for being gay, without recourse. There's no protection for discrimination—though that's going to change with the new Congress."

A different type of stadium star, singer Clay Aiken, parried a question from Diane Sawyer on "Good Morning America":

Sawyer: For three years now, everyone has assumed the right to ask if Clay Aiken [is] gay? Everybody assumed that what has really been happening in these last few years with you and what's probably going to happen right here today, in this next couple of weeks, is that you are ready to come out and say you're gay.

Aiken: That would not make any sense for me to do that.

Not long afterward, on "Larry King Live," when the host asked him "hypothetically" if it would affect his career if he were gay, he responded "hypothetically, I don't think so."

A longtime target of Web gossip, Aiken has become adept at

deflecting questions about his sexuality—often by phrasing his answers as questions. But when a man came forward last year professing to have hooked up with Clay for sex after responding to an ad, the press went wild ("Clay Is Gay," trilled the *National Enquirer*). As other celebrities have discovered, in cyberspace no one can hear your denials. Lance Bass and Neil Patrick Harris broke out of glass last year partly because of intensive Web chatter, and neither seems the least bit hurt by his emergence.

But at least—yeah, there's that phrase again—he hardly denies it anymore. Maybe Clay figures that takes him a step away from his most famous song title, "Invisible."

Surprisingly enough, the concept of being semi-sort-of-out has even infiltrated the ranks of the Republicans. Pioneer outing journalist Michelangelo Signorile feels that "in the Republican Party now, the glass closet is okay. It's like 'just don't talk about it or announce it.' It's progress, but it also still makes being gay something you really shouldn't talk about." But things got extra sticky when people started asking questions about then Republican National Committee chairman Ken Mehlman's sexuality. At first, Mehlman refused to answer any questions, which only fueled the discussion, until he flatly told a *New York Daily News* reporter, "I'm not gay." The fact that he parried the question for so long, wrote Washington blogger John Aravosis, was in itself unusual. "I can't recall many, if any, straight men who refuse to acknowledge that they're straight—if anything, most are a bit too obvious about it—and that ultimately leads to speculation, caused by Mehlman's own failure to respond to a direct question posed by a reporter."

Keeping the glass up is a high-maintenance job, especially since many celebs are left to do it—or, more often, screw it up—alone. Bragman swears there are no meetings between stars and their handlers to strategize whether or not they will stay glassed off. That would explain the various slipups that happen when the luminaries take their own images by the balls. I was wildly amused some years ago when the terminally noncommittal Sean Hayes was asked by a newspaper interviewer what he likes in a partner and he blurted out that he's "not into that gay ideal of musclemen." This from the guy who refuses to label his sexuality. Whoopsy! (Though he can always say "Well, I said I'm not into the gay ideal.") Meanwhile, the more circumspect David Hyde Pierce is quoted on the Internet Movie Database as saying, "My life is an open book, but don't expect me to read it to you."

I also loved the blind item in the *New York Post* a few years ago about how a more calculating star goes into premiere screenings with his female date while his male trainer enters separately and, when the lights go down, switches seats to be next to the star. Good try—but obviously the charade was shabby enough to eventually make it into print.

A popular argument in favor of celebs not going on the record with their gayness is that these people deserve privacy, after all. "It's nobody's business but theirs," onlookers counter—usually while devouring a trashy tabloid.

It's true that stars are free to put up whatever walls they want in order to maintain boundaries with the public. But even at their most controlling, straight stars never seem to leave out the fact that they're straight in interviews. Whenever a subject tells me, "I won't discuss who I'm dating" or "I resent labels," I generally know not so much that they're passionate about privacy but that they're gay, gay, gay.

Are the glassy—or ambiguous—stars tortured? Sometimes. It must be weird to be, say, Wanda Sykes and turn up with gal pals at New York City's gay lounge Beige and at Fire Island discos while seeming to exude a hope that no one notices enough to ask whether you are or aren't. But if played right, there are benefits to the high-wire act. As Signorile disdainfully puts it, "Anderson Cooper has finessed it where straight women who have a crush on him think he's straight and gay men actually think he's out. [The glass closeters] are able to play to different niche audiences whatever sexual orientation those people want, and they believe it!"

Once again, bravo! (said with rolling eyes). When halfheartedness is used as a career move, there's little to cheer about, especially when truthin' could be the road to real relief. As newfound lesbian Cynthia Nixon told *New York* magazine after coming out, "If someone is chasing you, stop running. And then they'll stop chasing you." So come on, people, just say the words. Or just mouth them. At least.

Menstruation: Porn's Last Taboo
Trixie Fontaine

"Will you pee for me?"

It was one of the first requests I got as a webwhore during a private webcam show, and I was happy to oblige my customer for $2.99 a minute. I grabbed a Tupperware bowl, aimed the cam at my pussy, and pissed until my bladder went dry. *Cha-ching!* I envisioned logging into the camsite every morning to empty my bladder and line my pockets. Who knew webwhoring could be so simple and the customers so easy to please?

A week later I found out it wasn't so simple; yellow shows were (and still are) against most camsites' rules and many camgirls' accounts had been closed for disobeying by spraying. I was flabbergasted—doesn't a piss ban on a porn site violate common sense? You can see men eating urine snow cones by going to your neighborhood video store and renting *Jackass: The Movie*, so what's wrong with videos of a sterile body fluid being streamed over the Internet to a porn consumer? I grudgingly stopped doing pee shows to avoid being kicked off the camsite, but the rationale of the no-piss rule eluded me.

Even more befuddling than the camsite's no-piss rule was the no-menstruation rule. What could possibly be wrong with me masturbating my own pussy at the wettest time of the month? Doing period shows seemed a lot more natural, less offensive, and safer than women doing the ever-popular (and camsite acceptable) extreme penetration shows, fucking themselves with baseball bats, footballs, and beer cans.

A year later I opened my own Internet porn site selling monthly memberships to people who wanted to see my spycams, photos, and videos. Owning my own site meant I was out from under the thumb of the big corporate camsites and could set my own rules. I did pee shows and integrated my period into shows like, "Bloody Body Painting" and photo sets like "Blood in the Studio." I enjoyed showing off my period not because I got any customer requests to see it, but because menstruation is so conspicuously absent from porn. I was determined that my porn site be honest about me, my sexuality, and my body—how could my site be genuine and real if I ignored and hid the fluid coursing through my cunt once a month? I didn't want my site to portray only the typical skewed porno version of women's bodies and sexuality; I can think of no greater misrepresentation of premenopausal women's bodies than having 100 percent of porn pretend that 15–25 percent of our vaginas' monthly experience just doesn't exist.

While none of my members requested to see me on the rag, they didn't complain when I shared my period with them. Some of them chose not to look at it because they couldn't handle blood, some of them said it didn't exactly turn them on but it was "interesting," and some of them just thought it was no big deal. I was happy my fans were tolerant and supportive, but I was still mystified by men's disproportionate interest in pee versus menstruation. It surprised me that guys were so much more interested in a fluid that comes out of our peeholes than one that comes exclusively out of women's pussies.

As it turns out, pee is more easily eroticized by men than menstrual fluid because pissing is something they can relate to and urine more closely resembles semen. The only association most men have with blood is pain. Even scat is far more popular and sought after among porn consumers than menstruation. In the world of Internet porn, chances are you'll run across more enema enthusiasts than menstruation enthusiasts. You will find more guys on the Web talking about how they want to give a chick's dirty asshole a tongue-bath than you will guys who want to eat bloody pussy. Of course, none of this makes rational sense since menstruation is literally the "sexiest" of these three bodily functions (peeing, pooping, and menstruating), since it's part of the reproductive process and menstrual fluid exits the body through the vagina.

After a while I found a menstruation fetish site run by Tuna, a man who commissioned period porn from amateurs like me. I was really excited to discover an eager (if small) market for the bloody photos and videos I wanted to make. The webmaster sent me a link to his page for models, describing the types of poses he wanted with sample pictures to illustrate what he was looking for. My excitement waned and transformed into disgust when I saw the emphasis was less on menstruating women and more on waste products: bloody maxi pads, anonymous twats with tampon strings, garbage cans with bloody tampons and panty liners, and a rear-end view of a woman with her panties pulled down to reveal a dripping tampon that had overflowed onto a pad.

My naïve fantasy of presenting menstruation as a natural, healthy and inoffensive occurrence worthy of integrating into sex and porn was overshadowed by images of things that belong in a landfill. I wanted to make period porn so people could start thinking of period sex as good clean fun, not to reinforce old perceptions of menstruation as something dirty and stinky. I wanted to display my period as a fresh, free-flowing, messy puddle of fun, not just something to be stifled and absorbed by a piece of garbage.

In spite of my distaste, I tackled my commissioned photo set with as much enthusiasm and creativity as I could, reminding myself that the webmaster was polite, generous with advertising, and couldn't be resented for fetishizing the one component of menstruation that's visible in our society: "feminine hygiene" products. A boy's first exposure to menstruation isn't wet red pussy, it's advertisements for tampons, it's the package of Kotex his mom keeps under the sink, it's his sister's used maxi beckoning mysteriously from the bathroom wastebasket. With most die-hard true "fetishists," a single thing or one small piece of the whole captures the attention of someone in immaturity and sticks with him as he grows and focuses on the thing, amplifies the thing, and sexualizes the thing. It could be white panties or high heels or armpits or rubber swim caps…or pads and tampons. Because a lot of women don't want to have sex while they're on the rag, observing her bulging panties or dangling strings, or inspecting used pads and tampons (and tampon applicators) are the closest their male partners ever get to experiencing the intimate details of menstruation.

Even if I didn't like the focus on "sanitary" napkins and tampons, I grew to enjoy catering to menstruation fetishists anyway. It didn't adhere to my ideal vision of period porn, but it did appeal to my nonconformist desire to make provocative porn, even if the main reaction I provoked was disgust. I've always enjoyed grossing people out and if that meant I could make money in an underserved niche by dripping blood into my mouth from my oversaturated tampons, it was fine with me. I liked confronting people with my body fluids and knew that even if my members didn't exactly like it, they would remember me for it. There was plenty of other noncontroversial content on my website to entertain them, so I felt that including the unique red content could only help establish my brand and set me apart from other solo girl paysites.

Unfortunately, it could also ruin my business.

Rather than get our own merchant accounts and infrastructure for processing payments online, most independent porn webmasters in the United States process credit card payments through a third party, CCBill. CCBill is now the most popular and trusted third party processor as others turned out to be unreliable and/or folded under new Visa regulations and restrictions deeming porn merchants "high-risk" accounts and requiring substantial registration fees. Not long after I started making period porn, CCBill suspended service on Tuna's account for violating their acceptable use policy. CCBill also stopped processing payments for the woman owned and operated the site, OnMyPeriod.com. When site owner May Ling Su couldn't find anything addressing menstruation in CCBill's posted acceptable use policy (besides restrictions on "extreme violence, incest, snuff, scat, mutilation, or rape"), she called to ask them where menstruation is mentioned in their AUP. May Ling Su says,

[As I was] talking on the phone with the people at CCBill, they explained to me that it falls under the bodily fluids and excretions clause. I asked them if they still provide services to sites containing male ejaculation. "Yes," he answered, "but that's different."

"How is it different?" I asked. "Sounds to me like sexual discrimination."

"I don't want to have a semantics argument with you," one of them started.

"No, you don't," I answered. "You won't win."

Even if they would entertain our arguments and we could prove that their policy equating menstruation with feces is primitive and discriminatory (their "Bodily Excretions" clause in its entirety forbids "any and all depictions and/or actual occurrences and/or references involving the content of, advertising or marketing of scat/fecal matter, and/or a woman's period or menstruation"), and even if they agreed that menstruation is a more normal function to integrate into sex play than, say, a gang of twenty guys ejaculating on a teenager's face or a woman being double- or triple-penetrated anally (bukkake, dp and tp are all "acceptable" in the porn world), CCBill is only bowing to the higher power of Visa who couldn't care less if they lose revenue from porn transactions; in spite of unsubstantiated reports about pornography being a multibillion-dollar industry, Visa could certainly live without Internet porn's drop-in-the-bucket sales and the high chargeback rates endemic in our industry.

With no reliable alternatives for processing payments, May Ling Su made her site free, Tuna turned to a European processor, and I held my breath hoping no one would rat me out to CCBill by telling them I had menstruation content tucked in between my softcore photo sets and striptease videos. Eventually I moved all of my red content to its own site, BloodyTrixie.com, to avoid having my white-bread-and-butter site's income compromised with CC-Bill (although I am still technically breaking their rules simply by providing a link to my red site).

I don't think any of us really blame CCBill for covering their asses with Visa and I doubt that they relish shutting people down. It may sound counterproductive, but I actually appreciate CCBill's conservativism; we all want to have a reliable payment processor that follows the rules, prevents fraudulent transactions and pays us on time, and we know the rules didn't start with CCBill or even with Visa. In fact, no one really knows *what* the rules are because obscenity laws are extremely vague and entirely subjective, varying from one community's set of standards to another's. As attorney Anthony Comparetto says, "the problem with obscenity is that it is the only crime in which you don't know when you have committed it. Think about that. You are driving down the road doing thirty-five miles an hour, and a police officer pulls you over to give you a speeding ticket. You tell him you were not speeding, and that there are no speed limit signs. He agrees that there are no speed limit signs, as it is up to the officer to determine if you are speeding…in his opinion. And you get the ticket."

The general public might assume laws against obscenity are just holdovers from bygone days, left on the books but never enforced, like laws against playing dominoes on Sunday or getting fish drunk. On the contrary, check out some of the steps made during George W. Bush's administration to combat obscenity:

- Under the guise of protecting children, in 2003 Congress enacted the Protect Act with an amendment authored by Republican congressman Tom Feeney restricting judges from imposing sentences lighter than suggested minimums even in cases involving obscenity that does not involve children.
- Record-keeping regulations (18 U.S.C. 2257) requiring porn producers to keep model IDs on file proving they were eighteen or over at the time of the shoot were revised to include a level of detailed documentation and disclosure that jeopardizes the privacy and safety of porn actors and models and is nearly impossible to maintain without error.
- Continuing the Ashcroft-declared war on pornography, in

May the Department of Justice announced the establishment of an Obscenity Prosecution Task Force (in addition to the already-existing Child Exploitation and Obscenity Unit).

With these kinds of steps being taken, we can expect the DOJ to file even more obscenity-related charges in communities specifically chosen for their conservative standards, increasing the likelihood of conviction. So what *are* community standards regarding sex acts involving menstruation? Judging from comments in online communities, both men and women are shocked by the censorfree area of BloodyTrixie.com, calling it "gross," "disgusting," and "disturbing." Even jaded adult webmasters accustomed to the most degrading hardcore porn imaginable respond to tame videos of intercourse with a menstruating woman by remarking, "Damn that is some sick shit. People who enjoy that fetish are really messed up," and "I've seen a lot in this biz but that's some really nasty shit. Why not just wait till it runs its course or get a blowjob? Takes unsafe sex to another level and generally it's not pleasant pussy."

On the other hand, plenty of people pipe up during forum discussions about period porn to say that they enjoy red sex and point out that the disgusted parties must not have a lot of experience with women if they're "afraid to get a little blood on their swords." On the legal front, the beginning of 2005 saw the U.S. Supreme Court kill the Feeney Amendment, and a District Court judge dismiss the charges as unconstitutional in this presidential administration's first high-profile obscenity case, filed against Extreme Associates. Of course, the DOJ appealed the judge's ruling, which stated that people's constitutional right to *possess* obscene materials is infringed upon by the government's ban on the sale and distribution of obscenity (making it impossible to possess obscenity unless you create it yourself).

The core values forming the foundation of the United States government's war on obscenity are the same as its core values opposing sex workers' rights across the board: they concede that sex itself is okay, but insist that it's *not* okay to actually *sell* sex. The government's antiporn warriors continually defend the persecution of pornographers by claiming to support First Amendment rights and privacy rights, essentially saying that we have the right to create and view obscenity…we just don't have the right to distribute it or make any money off of it. We women (just barely) have the right to do what we want with our bodies, as long as we don't make money on it. In fact, the sentences for obscenity *increase* based on how much money you've profited on through your "crime"; instead of being congratulated and sheltered from prosecution for your capitalistic ways as a good war profiteer, timber tycoon, or pharmaceutical company would be, the severity of your punishment increases proportionate to the amount of revenue you generate through sex.

We're encouraged to pay plastic surgeons to "beautify" our labia and stuff our cheeks, tits, and asses with implants, but we're breaking the law if we charge men money to fuck our cosmetically modified cunts. We're encouraged to pay tens of thousands of dollars to fertility therapists and remain on bed rest for months so we can distend our wombs with litters of artificially conceived babies, but if we sell pictures of ourselves with our girlfriend's hand in our twats we could be fined and go to prison for distributing the obscenity of fisting. We're encouraged to buy feminine hygiene products from "respectable" corporations like Proctor & Gamble, Johnson & Johnson, and Kimberly-Clarke, generating over fourteen billion pads, tampons and applicators for North American landfills per year, but God forbid we charge anyone money to watch videos of us actually using one of these products. We're encouraged to buy hundreds (if not thousands) of dollars worth of pills individually to cope with menstrual cramps under a system that makes health care unaffordable for the average indie webwhore, but if we earn money by selling explicit videos demonstrating cramp reduction by masturbating ourselves to a juicy red orgasm we could find ourselves behind bars.

Menstruation may be the last taboo, but being a whore is the first...and we *still* haven't conquered that one. Before we can expect people to accept eroticized menstruation (or golden showers or fisting or a host of other "extreme" consensual sexplay elements) we must demand the basic right to sell sex in general. The current administration and its anti-obscenity posses are on the lookout for people like me, the kinds of people who turn public sentiment against the sex industry by our kinky ventures out of the mainstream, creating easy targets for precedent-setting court cases they can use later to further limit sex workers offering more vanilla fare. Is it worth it to make a big red target of myself and the industry in general just to assert that I should be able to do whatever I want with my menstruating pussy AND make money while I do it? Maybe I'm doing more harm than good, anyway; while failing to ever depict women menstruating in porn is a gross misrepresentation of our bodies, porn that caters to many red fetishists (e.g., "tampon munching teens") is also misrepresentative of the average menstruating woman's experiences—do I really want to pave the way for more male pornographers to jump on the red wagon and populate the Web with their own ignorant, exploitative versions of menstruation?

Who am I kidding? The Internet is going to be littered with degrading, twisted, and moronic porn whether I'm present on it or not. The religious right is going to condemn us and sic their Rethuglicans on us whether I stay put or pussy out. The conservative element in government doesn't distinguish between sex

workers except from a strategic standpoint in their efforts to eradi-
cate *all* of us. Sex work has to be validated and legalized across the
board; our rights won't be won by segregating our ranks between
least-offensive and most-offensive, so I'm just going to keep on of-
fending in whatever ways sound like fun.

Buying Obedience: My Visit to a Pro Submissive

Greta Christina

Part One: Thinking about It

First of all—no, the book didn't give me the idea. I've thought about hiring a professional submissive for years, long before the book came along. I've thought about it idly, fantasized about it intensely, even read the ads in the back of the adult papers with semiserious intent. But the book is what gave me the courage, or maybe just the excuse, to go ahead and actually do it.

A quick explanation. See, I recently edited this book, *Paying for It: A Guide by Sex Workers for Their Clients,* which is pretty much what it sounds like—a collection of writing by sex workers, with advice for customers on how to treat sex pros so they like you and give you a better time. I edited the book (and wrote parts of it myself) very much from the point of view of the worker, and while it was written with sympathy and compassion for the customer, it was written entirely in the workers' voices.

But as soon as I started working on the book, I started wondering: what would it be like on the other side?

Part of my interest was professional. How easy would it be, I wondered, to follow the advice in my own book? Would having the guidelines make me feel relaxed and confident about hiring a sex pro? Or would they make me even more anxious about whether I was doing it right?

But mostly, I was just curious. Sexually curious, I mean, not just intellectually curious. What would be different about getting off with someone who was doing it for the money, instead of doing it pro bono? I liked the idea of paying someone so I could have the session be about me me me, so I could be sexually selfish without feeling guilty. That's a big reason I decided to hire a submissive instead of an escort or a dominant—it fit so beautifully into that fantasy. But would it really be like that? Would I really be able to think of her as my servant girl, there for the sole purpose of doing my bidding and getting me off? Or would I be unable to let go of my reflex of wanting her to like me, wanting her to think I was cool, wanting her to have fun too?

And would the very fact of the money get in the way? Would it make me mistrust my own instincts? Would the money be constantly in my mind, a nagging reminder that she probably wouldn't be there if she didn't have bills to pay? I knew from the writing in *Paying for It* (and from my own experience as a stripper) that sex workers do sometimes like their customers and sometimes even get off with them. But weirdly, knowing this wasn't entirely comforting. It made me want to prove myself, made me want to be one of those special ones…which, of course, made it harder to imagine just selfishly letting myself be catered to. Would I be able to forget about the money? And if not, would I be able to let the money be part of the power dynamic, one of the things that made the encounter unique and hot?

There was only one way to find out.

Part Two: Planning It

I'll tell you this right off the bat. As soon as I started even think-ing about hiring a pro, I immediately got a lot more sympathy for sex customers. I even got more sympathy for some of those cus-tomers' more common failings. See, as soon as I started imagining hiring a submissive, I of course started having sex fantasies about it—and one of my first fantasies was about the woman dropping her professional limits for me and making an exception to the "no sex" rule that most pro submissives have.

Now, dealing with customers who push their sex workers to do off-limits stuff is one of the big pet peeves in the industry; it's an absolute top-notch way for a customer to be an asshole. But now I'm not sure it is about being an asshole. I don't think it's about be-ing a selfish jerk who wants what she wants and doesn't care how the other person feels. Or at least, it's not always about that.

I think it's about wanting to be special. It's about wanting to not be just another customer, wanting to be the one the pro likes so much that she (or he) will make an exception and in-vite you across that line. For me, the pro sub in my fantasies al-ways made the exception because I was a woman—either the "no sex" rule didn't apply to girls, or she was so excited about playing with a woman that she let the rule slide. As if lesbian erotic sis-terhood was so powerful that it rendered professional limits ob-solete. I knew rationally that this was absurd, but it was a very difficult fantasy to let go of. And it was hard not to feel disap-pointed about it, even before I'd booked the session. I still think pushing sex workers to do off-limits stuff is a top-notch way to be an asshole—but I now have more sympathy for the impulse.

And once I stopped just thinking about it and started actually shopping around for a pro submissive, my sympathy for customers went sky high. It was a weirdly nerve-wracking experience, a blend of comparison shopping and answering a personal ad. I wanted to come across as respectful and experienced and interesting and fun: if for no other reason, I knew that sex workers do sometimes turn down customers, and I wanted to look like a good prospect. At the same time, I wanted to be sure I was getting the best person available for my desires, or at least some assurance that I'd actually be getting what I was paying for. To put it bluntly, I wanted to get my money's worth. And while as a former sex worker I'm happy to advise customers, "If you don't hit it off with a sex worker, write it off to bad luck and try again with someone else," that advice was tough to accept when it was my own hard-earned, not-very-plentiful cash on the line.

It might have been different if I'd been looking for an escort or a dominatrix. Those fields have a glut of professionals to choose from (in the San Francisco area, at least), and shopping for someone with compatible interests, good energy, and hot photos would probably have been pretty easy. But there aren't a jillion people doing professional submission, even in the Bay Area. So while my filthy sex fantasies involved sorting through a large online harem of beauties and picking the one who most suited my whims, the reality was that my choices were limited.

To make things more difficult on myself, I wanted to hire someone with a lot of experience in professional submission, not just a domme who switched now and then on the side. And for reasons that are somewhat obscure even to me, I didn't want to go to one of these brothel-y domination houses if I didn't have to. I'm probably not being fair, but the houses seemed too much like an assembly line, and nowhere near private enough. I wanted someone who worked for herself…which of course narrowed my choices even further. It wasn't a problem exactly—the few independent pro subs I did find seemed perfectly good—but I hadn't realized how much of my fantasy was about the power of selection until I discovered how little selection there was. And the limited options made me that much more anxious to make a good impression when I did make my choice.

I decided to go with Rachel, of www.rachelobeys.com (no longer online, alas). Her website was expressive and articulate, with plenty of details about do's and don'ts as well as about her general style. Her vibe seemed submissive and eager to please, and at the same time clear and firm about limits. And—I felt guilty about being this shallow, but there it was—her body was more my type. Voluptuous rather than skinny, with big boobs and a round, spankable ass. That wasn't my top consideration, but it certainly wasn't my most trivial one either—and with so little info to go on, it became even more central. I set up an anonymous email account, took a deep breath, and dropped her a line.

And the minute I started composing my email, my first question was answered: yes, I was glad to have the guidebook in my hand. True, the book did give me a certain amount of "Am I doing this right?" performance anxiety, what with knowing all those damn guidelines and wanting to be good about following them. But I'd have had performance anxiety no matter what. That's just the kind of gal I am. And while the book did give my anxiety some very concrete forms, it also gave me the tools to cope. My stomach had serious butterflies—during every step of the process, actually, not just this first one—but at least my head was saying, "You're doing fine, you're doing everything you're supposed to."

More importantly, I'd have been a lot more shy about spelling out my specific desires if I hadn't been assured by every damn writer in *Paying for It* that spelling out specific desires is exactly what sex workers want you to do. They don't want to play guessing games, and they don't want you leaving disappointed and pissed just because they couldn't read your mind. This makes perfect common sense, of course; but it still felt a little weird to provide a total stranger with a short but detailed list of my sexual expectations. It was good to have a clear, authoritative consensus telling me to go ahead and do exactly that.

And spelling out what I was looking for wound up handing me an extremely pleasant surprise. I knew I shouldn't expect sex from a professional submissive; and sure enough, Rachel had "no sex" clearly stated on her website. But since every person on the planet seems to define "sex" differently, I thought I should check with her about what, exactly, she meant by this.

"I understand and respect the 'no sex' rule," I said in my email, "and would absolutely stay within your limits. But…" and I proceeded to ask about a few specifics, which she might or might not consider sex. Ordering her to masturbate. Caressing or squeezing her bottom while I spanked her. Caressing or squeezing her breasts before putting clamps on them. Masturbating while I looked at her. Masturbating while I spanked her, or while I fondled her ass. I put this list in my email, fully expecting her to say "No" to most or all of it, and half-afraid that even asking would make her blow me off as a clueless oaf who didn't get that pro submission isn't prostitution. I waited fretfully, obsessively checking my email, increasingly certain with each passing hour that I'd blown it and would have to start from scratch with someone else.

But Rachel finally replied…and I couldn't have been more wrong. Not only was everything I wanted okay with her, but a number of things I wouldn't have asked for in a bezillion years turned out to be okay as well. I could fondle and even chew on her breasts; I could rub my cunt against her ass; I could spank her pussy with my bare (gloved) hand. I could even "masturbate" her if I wanted to. That one really took me by surprise. In Lesbian-land where I come from, we call that "fingering," and it's without question considered sex. But I wasn't about to argue. The only things that were off-limits were body-fluid-exchange stuff like fucking and sucking, and I could happily live without those for an hour.

So the moral of the story is, ask your sex professional for what you want. But even if it had turned out the other way—if all the extras I'd wanted had been off-limits—I still would have been glad I'd asked. As much as I'd have hated to miss a pleasure because I didn't know it was permitted, I'd have hated even more to try something and have it turn out to be verboten. And if I hadn't asked ahead of time about this "borderline" stuff, I doubt I'd have had the nerve to try any of it.

Of course, now that Rachel and I had discussed details and scheduled a date, both my fantasies and my fretfulness were in sharp, vivid focus. I spent the days before the session veering between high anxiety and near-blinding horniness; between insistent, poorly timed fantasies about the session, and a displaced fretfulness over details: what to wear, what to bring, how to get there, what if I missed my train, what if the dungeon caught fire. An hour before the session, all my planning and fantasizing and blocking out the broad strokes of the session had gone completely blank, replaced by teeth-grinding obsession over minutiae and a loud buzzing in my head. I kept chanting to myself, "This is for me, this is for my pleasure, I'm doing this for myself"...a mantra that utterly failed to sink in. And fifteen minutes before the session, everything in my brain had been obliterated by the blank, terrified hyperawareness that I was trying to find my way through a strange, slightly dicey neighborhood with three hundred dollars cash in my wallet.

Also, did my hair look okay?

Part Three: Doing It

Did I mention the fretfulness, the anxiety, the blank terror? All of it focused into a laser beam of panic when I rang the doorbell and walked through the dungeon door. I'm tempted to say that it felt like crossing a line, like stepping across a border into unknown and forbidden territory that I could never return from unchanged. All of which is true, it did feel like that, except I was also aware of what a dorky, overdramatic metaphor that was. Mostly, I just had no fucking idea what to do next.

But Rachel, of course, was a professional. She knew how to put nervous horny people at ease, and she knew what to do next. She graciously took my money, and she sat me on the sofa and chatted a bit about what we'd be doing, and she walked me around the dungeon showing me her toys…and while part of me was watching the clock tick and wondering, "Am I paying for this?", a much larger part was relieved to have the chance to get my bearings. I was getting a sense of the physical space, which was helping me relax and settle in…and which was giving me ideas.

And of course, now I knew what Rachel looked like. Yes, I'd seen photos on her website, but we all know about photos. They can lie in so many ways, not least of which are the lies you tell yourself when you look at them. But while Rachel didn't look exactly the way I'd imagined—she was taller, and dressed more conventionally—I certainly wasn't disappointed. If anything, her photos didn't do her justice. So by the time the tour was over, I was…not relaxed exactly, but no longer paralyzed. And while I was still deeply weirded out, I was also getting a little turned on.

So we started. Slowly at first. I sat in a wooden chair, crossed my legs, and told her to stand in front of me while I looked at her. Then to turn around while I looked at her. Then to bend at the waist, pull up her skirt, and slowly pull down her panties while I looked at her. All of this was familiar territory, and for the first time that day, I began to feel like I actually was in control.

So I was watching this pretty, sexy, obedient woman bend over with her skirt hiked up and her panties pulled down, when it occurred to me that it might be fun to go squeeze her butt. Immediately I thought, "No. Not yet. You were going to wait for that." (I wasn't kidding about blocking out the session beforehand. In my hyperanxious state, I'd been worried that if I didn't, I'd get lost in the preliminaries and wouldn't have time for the main events.)

But then it dawned on me: "Screw that. This is for you. The whole idea is that this is for you. She's a submissive: she's here to do what you want, when you want it. So to hell with your stupid timeline. If your clit wants you to squeeze her ass, then go squeeze her ass." (I guess my "This is for you" mantra had sunk in after all.) I walked over behind her, let my hand hover above her bare ass for a moment, and touched her.

And that, more than walking through the dungeon door, is what made me feel like I'd crossed a line. Touching the naked skin of someone whom I'd paid for the pleasure, squeezing her flesh while my clit throbbed and then squeezing it harder to make my clit throb again…that is what made me feel like I'd done something I couldn't take back, become somebody I couldn't change. It was unnerving—but it was also exciting, in the way that adventure is always exciting. And now that I'd unequivocally stepped into this strange place, now that I wasn't just freaking out trying to imagine what it might be like, it began to feel less strange, and my confidence grew with every squeeze of my hand and twitch of my clit.

I began to take things a little further. I made Rachel show me her breasts, and then groped them. I made her crawl on the floor, and then followed her around groping her ass while she crawled. I switched back and forth between touching her and watching her: between using her for the pleasure of my hands and using her for the pleasure of my eyes, between treating her like a sex toy and treating her like a piece of pornography.

Now normally, if I were feeling like this in an S/M scene, I'd start telling my partner about it, so she could get off on her objectification as much as I was. I was about to do that with Rachel. But then I thought: "No. I want to be lazy. *I* know that I'm thinking of her as a sex toy, and I'm getting off on it. I don't need her to know it, too. I just need her to keep doing it." I was starting to get into this whole selfish "you are here solely to serve my needs" thing, and I wanted to go with it.

But being sexually selfish turned out to be much harder than I'd anticipated. I hadn't quite realized this before, but apparently a lot of what I get off on as a top is feedback: the admiration of my wonderful skill and sensitivity and general toppy hotness. It was extremely difficult to not care about whether Rachel thought I was hot. And even though I was playing the whole "distant and cool" thing as a sexual game, I think I was also doing it as a defense. I knew that no matter how Rachel was responding to me, I'd be wondering if it was real or an act she was getting paid to put on. Playing the "this is all about me" game meant I didn't have to think about that question.

It was still hard, though. And it got harder as the scene got more physical. When I took Rachel over my knee and started spanking her, I had to remind myself of our email negotiations, and the fact that she'd made a point of telling me, several times, that I should feel free to spank her. I knew in my head that she was okay with being spanked. She'd shown me a whole cabinet of paddles and crops and floggers I could use on her, of course she was okay with being spanked. In fact, it sounded from her emails like she was a lot more than okay with being spanked. But paying somebody to let me physically hurt them still took some adjustment.

And even when I was getting into the selfishness game, part of what I selfishly wanted was a certain kind of response. It took me an embarrassingly long time to figure out that I could ask for that as well. I could order her to wriggle or be still when I spanked her, to moan or be quiet, to beg me to stop or to beg for more. But once I let go of my worry over whether she was faking, I realized how much pleasure I found in telling her how to react. It was an unsettling pleasure, but an intense one: the power I felt in controlling, not just her behavior, but her response to mine.

I'll say this for damn sure: It was wonderful to be able to spank her as hard as I wanted. I'm not sure I've ever spanked anyone as hard as I wanted. Rachel liked being spanked, and she liked it hard, and I could spank her as hard as I could, for as long as I liked. I could spank her until my hand hurt, and then spank her more when my hand recovered. I could squeeze or tickle her ass after a good hard series of whacks…and when I got bored doing that, I could start spanking her again, as soon as I felt like it. Or I could grope her breast with one hand while I spanked her with the other, getting off on the feel of her tits without worrying about whether I was doing it exactly right. Of all the things we did in the session, bending Rachel over my knee and spanking her was the closest I came to really experiencing the fantasy: the closest I came to really feeling like I was being serviced by an obedient submissive whose only purpose was to comply with my orders and get me off.

As the scene became more intense, the whole "it's all about me" game got easier. Yet at the same time, it got more perplexing. When

I was doing something that required care and delicacy, like spanking Rachel between her legs, I'd be intently focused on not harming her or pushing too hard—while at the same time, I'd be cruelly trying to maximize her pain and frustration, making her play with her clit to get it excited and swollen before I started hitting it again. When I was doing things that to me felt blatantly sexual, like rubbing my cunt against her ass while I groped her tits and masturbated with a vibrator, I'd be paying strict attention to the details of her "no sex" limits—while at the same time, I'd be luxuriating in how dirty and fucked-up it felt to selfishly use this woman's body to get myself off. My top persona became colder, my orders coming in an increasingly chilly voice, accompanied by snapped fingers and an impatient bark when they weren't immediately followed. I got more comfortable with it, and more deeply into it, with each passing minute.

But it was still hard. Which is probably why I did what I did at the end of the session. I was pretty much done—to be crude about it, I'd finished coming—and I said to Rachel, "You've been very good. I've enjoyed this very much, and I want to give you a reward. Is there something you want before we finish? Something you want to do, or want me to do?"

"Honestly?" she asked. Her voice wasn't submissive or meek this time: it was straightforward and firm, and she didn't pause for even a second before asking.

"Yes."

She didn't hesitate. "I want to be spanked some more."

I smiled. "Do you like it hard?"

"Yes," she answered immediately, almost interrupting. "I like to be spanked hard."

I was so glad I'd asked. I had hoped that would be her answer. Her obvious enthusiasm relieved any residual guilt I had about the whole "selfishly hurting you and using you for my own erotic whims" thing. Besides, I really just wanted to spank her some more. I bent her over my lap again and started spanking, ordering her to beg me for it, to tell me how badly she wanted it. When I started worrying if I was doing it too hard, I reminded myself that this was what she'd specifically asked for, the thing she wanted more than anything, and I bucked up my courage and spanked her even harder. I kept it up, solid and relentless, until our time was almost up.

Then I ordered her onto the floor, on her back with her legs apart and her fingers spreading her cunt. I watched her silently for a minute, trying to fix the image in my brain. And I said, "That's it. We're done."

And then—boom. As soon as I said, "We're done," all the anxiety and paralysis came rushing back home. I was at a total loss about what to do next, almost as much as I'd been before the session started. I felt overwhelmed with social awkwardness: I had no idea how to make a two-minute transition from dom/sub roles into regular people roles…not that I knew what our "regular people" relationship was anyway. Rachel got dressed, sat me down on the sofa with her to chat, and asked if it was okay to cuddle for a minute.

Now, this is going to make me sound like a complete asshole, but an honest answer would have been "No." I didn't want to cuddle. I didn't even want to chat. I was feeling anxious and freaked out, and what I wanted was to give her my tip, say "Thank you," and get the hell out of there. But the scene was over: she wasn't my submissive servant anymore, we were social equals again, and after everything we'd been doing, saying "No" seemed churlish and rude. So I said "Sure," and put my arm around her stiffly while we chatted about the scene. I took off as soon as I gracefully could, and headed back to BART, thinking: *Boy, sex work is weird.*

Part Four: Analyzing It to Death Afterward

So here's the big, meaningful conclusion I've come to:

Boy, sex work is weird.

I don't mean that it's bad. I don't mean that it's sinful or exploitative or un-feminist, or any of that. But it's deeply, deeply weird. And being a customer felt much weirder than I'd ever felt as a provider. It was radically different from unpaid sex, much more so than I'd expected. It was as different from unpaid sex as S/M is from vanilla sex, as different as making love with a beloved partner is from fucking a stranger.

Why was it so different? It wasn't the "playing with a stranger" part so much: I've done that before, at sex parties and such. And it wasn't the "planning and scheduling sex in advance" part, either: I've done that before as well, with both long-term lovers and casual personal-ad hookups. But the combination of the two—making a definite, fairly detailed plan to have sex with someone that I'd never even met before—was deeply surreal. Even with strangers at sex parties, I'd known them for at least thirty seconds, had a chance to see if there was immediate physical chemistry, before deciding to boink them. This blend of careful calculation and blind leaping-into-the-abyss adventure was very peculiar indeed.

And of course, I was three hundred dollars poorer at the end of it, which isn't an insignificant difference. The money made me feel entitled to ask for what I wanted and (within reason) to get it. But it also made me feel pressured, like I had to cram as much pleasure as I could into the session to make it worth what I'd spent. And inevitably, it made me compare the experience to other luxuries, trying to judge whether that one hour had really been as good as thirty expensive cocktails, or ten pairs of Merino wool tights, or three fancy dinners out with my lover.

But the biggest difference between playing for money and

playing for free turned out to be the clock. Rachel had informed me ahead of time that she rented the dungeon by the hour and we had to be out by 8:00 p.m. sharp. Even if she hadn't, I didn't have the money to extend the session past the hour we'd scheduled. So I was constantly keeping an eye on the clock: winding up the spanking so we could get to the cunt torture, deciding not to use the flogger because we wouldn't have time to do it right. Now, I've certainly had quickies with a casual eye on the clock, have begun play sessions that we had to either cut short or miss our dinner reservations. But I'd never before played with anyone who was going to kick me out after exactly one hour, no matter what was going on or how much fun either of us was having. And this, I think, more than anything else about the session, made it nearly impossible for me to relax and just experience the moment.

I want to say something, though, and I want to say it very clearly: None of this weirdness or anxiety had anything to do with Rachel. Rachel was great. She knew her stuff, and she responded beautifully to my orders, and she was lovely to look at and luscious to fondle and spank. Any stress or distance I felt came from my own brainwaves and neuroses. Rachel did not make this a weird experience—I did.

Would I do it again? Well, if money were no object…but that's ridiculous. Of course money is an object. Money is *the* object, the whole point of the exercise, the thing that makes paying for it different from just surfing the personals for no-strings sex. So let me rephrase that. If I could afford it—if I weren't working a low-paying hippie-anarchist day job, if I hadn't recently paid for a big wedding and bought a house (and before you ask: yes, my wife knows about my adventure, and she's fine with it)—is this a luxury I'd save up for again?

I'm not sure. I had a good time, no question. I walked home

after the session with that loose, rumpled, hormone-addled strut people get when they've just gotten it good, as high and relaxed on my way back as I'd been freaked out and high strung on my way there. But it was a very weird good time, an awkward good time during much of it, and in many ways a deeply unsettling good time. And while I definitely got off, it didn't shake me to my core. The cool and distant persona I'd been cultivating was as much removed from herself as she was from Rachel, and her core was pretty damn unshakable. Besides, it's hard for my core to be shaken by someone I barely know.

But I have no idea how much of this unease and disconnect was simply unfamiliarity and first-time nerves. It's entirely possible that if I did it again, with experience under my belt and without feeling all anxious and ignorant and self-consciously transgressive, I'd have an even better time.

And in fact, I find that I'm still fantasizing about seeing a pro submissive. Not so much about the session I actually had; instead, I'm fantasizing about what I might do next time. I'm imagining what it'd be like if I let go of my fixation on being selfish and asked for more feedback; and I'm imagining what it'd be like if I could quit worrying about her responses and really let myself be selfish and cruel. And I'm wondering how the reality would stack up to the fantasy the second time around. So if money weren't such an obstacle, then yes. I'd probably do it again.

If only to find out what it was like.

About the Authors

AMY ANDRE has a master's degree in human sexuality studies from San Francisco State University. She works as a sex educator and writer.

VIOLET BLUE is the best-selling, award-winning author and editor of over a dozen books on sex and sexuality, all currently in print, a number of which have been translated into several languages; she has contributed to a number of nonfiction anthologies. Violet is a sex educator who lectures at the University of California and community teaching institutions, and writes about erotica, pornography, sexual pleasure, and health for major publications and blogs. She is a professional sex blogger and femmebot; an author at Metroblogging San Francisco (Metblogs); a correspondent for Geek Entertainment Television; she is on the Gawker payroll as girl friday contributor and editor at Fleshbot; in January 2007,

Violet was named a Forbes Web Celeb 25. She is a San Francisco native and human blog.Violet is the sex columnist for the *San Francisco Chronicle* with a weekly column titled "Open Source Sex," and has a podcast of the same name that frequents iTunes' top ten.

RICHARD BUSKIN is the *New York Times* best-selling author of more than a dozen nonfiction books on subjects ranging from Marilyn Monroe and Princess Diana to the Beatles and Sheryl Crow. The coauthor of comic Phyllis Diller's critically acclaimed autobiography, he is presently collaborating on the memoir of Loretta and Linda Sánchez, the only ever sisters to serve in Congress. Richard's articles have appeared in newspapers such as the *New York Post*, the *Sydney Morning Herald*, the *Observer*, and the *Independent*, and he also writes features and reviews for music and film magazines around the world. A native of London, England, he lives in Chicago.

GRETA CHRISTINA has been writing professionally since 1989. She is currently editing the annual *Best Erotic Comics* series, the first volume of which comes out in November 2007. She is editor of the anthology *Paying for It: A Guide by Sex Workers for Their Clients,* and author of the erotic novella *Bending,* which appeared in the three-novella collection *Three Kinds of Asking for It* edited by Susie Bright. Her writing has appeared in numerous magazines, newspapers, and anthologies, including *Ms., Penthouse,* the *Skeptical Inquirer,* and two volumes of the *Best American Erotica* series. She blogs at http://gretachristina.typepad.com/.

JEN CROSS is a smut writer and writing workshop facilitator, and is a co-collaborator in the dyke erotica collective, Dirty Ink. Her writing has appeared in a plethora of anthologies, including, most recently, *Nobody Passes, Best Women's Erotica 2007,*

Naughty Spanking Stories from A to Z 2, as well as on CleanSheets. com. She's featured at a number of San Francisco open mics, participated in the smutty part of LitQuake 2006's LitCrawl, and, because she cannot get enough words, also co-facilitates (with Carol Queen!) a monthly Erotic Reading Circle. As a queer incest survivor, Jen writes to release, transform, and create space for as much unspoken erotic as possible. For more information, visit www.writingourselveswhole.org.

MIRIAM DATSKOVSKY is a journalist and writer based in New York City. She got her start as the "Sexplorations" columnist for the *Columbia Daily Spectator,* for which she was featured in the *New York Times, Philadelphia Weekly*, and National Public Radio. In between busting her butt for a combined degree in political science and human rights studies from Barnard College, Miriam somehow found the time to serve as the *Spectator*'s editorial page editor. During her tenure she was responsible for expanding the section from five to seven pages a week and managing nearly thirty associate editors, writers, and artists. Miriam's work has also been featured in *New York* magazine. She is currently working on her first book (fingers crossed).

JILL EISENSTADT is the author of the novels *From Rockaway* and *Kiss Out* and is cowriter and producer on the 2006 feature film *The Limbo Room.* Her shorter work has appeared extensively in the *New York Times* and other places, including *Vogue, Elle, Mademoiselle,* and *Bomb* magazines. She lives in Brooklyn with her husband, the writer Michael Drinkard, and their three daughters.

DR. PARI ESFANDIARI is a native of Iran who now lives in California. An eyewitness to the Islamic Revolution, she left Iran shortly after. Esfandiari came face-to-face with postrevolution Iran and the condition of women when she returned to Iran sixteen years later. The experience led her to found Irandokht.com, a global media outlet that reflects the voices of Iranian Women. Esfandiari is a social entrepreneur and a business ethicist with over twenty years of diverse experience. She has a PhD in business ethics from the United Kingdom's Oxford Brookes University, and serves on the board of several nonprofit organizations in California. Her popular weekly television and radio programs about Middle-Eastern socio-political issues earned her the runner-up prize for the New American Media's 2004 Award in broadcast journalism. She is a public speaker and a frequent guest commentator on radio and television.

PAUL FESTA's sex essays appear in Nerve, Salon, *Best Sex Writing 2005* and *Best Sex Writing 2006*. His movie *Apparition of the Eternal Church,* about the music of Olivier Messiaen, was named Best North American Independent Feature Film at the 2006 Indianapolis International Film Festival. He is currently revising a novel and can be found online at paulfesta.com.

TRIXIE FONTAINE is a self-professed webwhore and Internet pornographer. She and her boy/girlfriend created and operate a handful of porn sites featuring themselves, including Trixie.com, SpyOnUs.com, and DeliaCD.com. Trixie is also an avid blogger/web-based diarist and much shorter in person than she appears on camera. Her boobs, however, are just as big and juicy in real life as they look in photos. In her spare time she likes to run her fingers across her stretch marks.

GAEL GREENE wrote "The Insatiable Critic" column for *New York* magazine for more than thirty years and remains on the staff, writing a weekly "Ask Gael" column. The author of *Blue Skies, No Candy; Doctor Love;* and other books, she is also cofounder (with James Beard) and board chair of Citymeals-on-Wheels, an organization that delivers 2.2 million meals a year to elderly housebound New Yorkers. She lives in New York City. Visit her at www.insatiable-critic.com.

MELISSA GIRA (melissagira.com) is a blogger, writer, editor of Sexerati: Smart Sex (sexerati.com), and a contributor to *Spread* magazine & the blogs BoundNotGagged, Gridskipper, and bub. blicio.us, "tracking the Web's social economy." An international sex worker rights' advocate, mobile media maker, and shameless sex futurist, she fully unpacked three times in the last year and prefers to work out of her purse-sized office: cell phone, wireless keyboard, and DV camera, wherever a cheap GPRS signal and fancy lip gloss can take her.

ASHLEA HALPERN is the associate features editor of *Time Out New York* magazine, and is the former sex columnist for the *Philadelphia City Paper.* Her work has appeared in *Maxim, Marie Claire, Glamour, Magnet, Bust, Cleveland Free Times, Detroit Metro Times, DIW, Skyscraper,* and *Punk Planet.* She lives in Brooklyn and shares custody of a nine-pound chihuahua.

KEVIN KECK is the author of *Oedipus Wrecked,* a collection of essays that features work first published on Nerve.com. He is also the father of three children who should be sufficiently embarrassed later in life by what he writes. Visit him at www.thekeck.com.

KELLY KYRIK has been writing professionally for over a dozen years. Her stories, essays, copy, and nonfiction articles have been printed in publications such as the *Chicago Tribune, Writer's Market, Cat Fancy,* and *Penthouse Forum.* She also writes several monthly columns, including one for *Police Magazine.* The subject matter of her writing runs the gamut; essays about marriage and family, how-to pieces for writers, sexually-themed articles and more. Samples of her writing can be seen at her website: www.kellykyrik.com.

As a freelance writer and columnist for sixteen years, LIZ LANG-LEY has covered subjects from a mini-golf course in a funeral home to the Global Orgasm for Peace. She's written for numerous magazines, newspapers and websites including Salon, *Glamour,* and alter-net.org. She is currently the pop culture columnist for the *Orlando Sentinel,* works with the Florida Film Festival, and teaches belly dancing.

ARIEL LEVY is a contributing editor at *New York* magazine where she writes about sexuality, culture and gender politics. She is the author of *Female Chauvinist Pigs.*

MICHAEL MUSTO writes the popular, long-running entertainment column "La Dolce Musto" in the *Village Voice.* He's also a contributor to *Out* magazine and a regular commentator on channels like MSNBC, E!, and VH1. In 2007, Carroll & Graf published *La Dolce Musto,* a collection of Musto's most zany and memorable columns through the years.

LUX NIGHTMARE has been obsessed with the Internet since 1994, obsessed with computers since 1987, and obsessed with sex since 1982. Career highlights include founding and running That Strange Girl (the first altporn site to feature both male and female models), interning at Nerve (back when it was cool), and keeping the masses educated about sex since 1997. She is the former features editor for Sexerati.com, a blog about sex, culture, and everything in between, and is working on a book about her years in the altporn scene.

Journalist, author, and screenwriter SCOTT POULSON-BRYANT studied at Brown University and was one of the founding editors of *VIBE* magazine. His journalism and essays have appeared in such publications as the *New York Times,* the *Village Voice, Rolling Stone* and *Spin.* His books include *What's Your Hi-Fi Q?* and *HUNG: A Meditation on the Measure of Black Men in America.* He is currently working on the first in a series of graphic novels. And yes, there's some sex involved.

KELLY ROUBA began her career as a writer before the start of her first journalism class. At the age of nineteen, Ms. Rouba was thrown into the fast-paced world of news reporting when she was hired as a stringer for a major area newspaper. With little experience beyond writing for her high school and middle school student newspapers, Ms. Rouba was determined to prove she could master the news beat. Now, after more than seven years, Ms. Rouba's passion for reporting the news is still evident as she continues to inform and entertain the public through her stories. She handles public relations projects and volunteers for several non-profit organizations.

RACHEL SHUKERT is a playwright and author based in New York City. Her plays include *Bloody Mary (*NYIT Award nominee), *The Red Beard of Esau, Sequins for Satan, The Blackstone Hotel,* and *Soiled Linens,* and have been produced and developed by Ars Nova, the Williamstown Theater Festival, the Culture Project, the

Ontological/Hysteric, the EVOLVE series at Galapagos, and the Omaha Lit Fest, among others.

Rachel is also a regular contributor to Nerve.com. She has also contributed to *Heeb* magazine, *McSweeney's,* Babble, Culturebot, and *Critical Moment.* Her upcoming collection of essays, *Have You No Shame?* will be published by Random House/Villard in the spring of 2008. Rachel holds a BFA from the Tisch School of the Arts at New York University. She was born and raised in Omaha, Nebraska.

TRISTAN TAORMINO (puckerup.com) is a columnist for the *Village Voice* and the author of *True Lust: Adventures in Sex, Porn and Perversion; Down and Dirty Sex Secrets;* and *The Ultimate Guide to Anal Sex for Women.* Her new book, *Opening Up: Creating and Sustaining Open Relationships, was* published in late 2007. She runs Smart Ass Productions, an adult film production company, and currently directs exclusively for Vivid Entertainment. Her award-winning titles for Vivid include *Chemistry* and *Tristan Taormino's Expert Guide to Anal Sex.* She teaches sex and relationship workshops around the world.

About the Editor

RACHEL KRAMER BUSSEL is a prolific erotica writer, editor, journalist, and blogger. She serves as senior editor at *Penthouse Variations,* hosts the In the Flesh Erotic Reading Series, and wrote the popular "Lusty Lady" column for the *Village Voice.* She's edited over a dozen erotic anthologies, including *Caught Looking: Erotic Tales of Voyeurs and Exhibitionism; Hide and Seek; Crossdressing: Erotic Stories; Naughty Spanking Stories from A to Z 1* and *2; First-Timers; Up All Night; Glamour-Girls: Femme/Femme Erotica; Ultimate Undies; Sexiest Soles; Secret Slaves: Erotic Stories of Bondage; Sex and Candy; Dirty Girls* and the kinky companion volumes *He's on Top* and *She's on Top* and *Yes, Sir* and *Yes, Ma'am.* Her first novel, *Everything But...* will be published by Bantam in summer 2008.

Her writing has been published in over one hundred anthologies, including *Best American Erotica 2004* and *2006, Everything You Know About Sex Is Wrong, Single State of the Union,* and *Desire: Women Write*

About Wanting, as well as *AVN, Bust,* Cleansheets.com, *Cosmo* UK, *Diva,* Fresh Yarn, Gothamist, Huffington Post, Mediabistro. com, Memoirville.com, *Newsday, New York Post,* Oxygen.com, *Penthouse, Playgirl, Punk Planet, San Francisco Chronicle, Time Out New York,* and *Zink.* Rachel has appeared on "The Berman and Berman Show," "Family Business," NY1, BBC, "Naked New York," and *"In the Life."* In her spare time, she hunts down the country's best cupcakes and blogs about them at cupcakestakethecake.blogspot.com. Visit her at www.rachelkramerbussel.com.